CELEBRATING CHRISTMAS

As If It Matters

CELEBRATING CHRISTMAS
As If It Matters

David Lambert

ZondervanPublishingHouse
Grand Rapids, Michigan

A Division of HarperCollins*Publishers*

Celebrating Christmas As If It Matters
Copyright © 1992 by David Lambert

Requests for information should be addressed to:
Zondervan Publishing House
Grand Rapids, Michigan 49530

Library of Congress Cataloging-in-Publication Data

Lambert, David (David Wesley), 1948–
    Celebrating Christmas as if it matters / David Lambert
       p. cm.
    ISBN 0-310-54441-6 (softcover)
    1. Christmas—United States. I. Title.
GT4986.A1L36   1992
394.2'68282'0973—dc20   92-11040
                                                              CIP

Edited by Evelyn Bence
Cover design by Tammy Grabrian Johnson
Cover photo by Jim Whitmer
Interior design by Bob Hudson

Printed in the United States of America

92 93 94 95 96 / CH / 5 4 3 2 1

For Cindy
My Spirit of Christmas Present and Future

God Bless Us, Every One

Contents

Preface

PARENTS FEEL ENOUGH GUILT at Christmas; it isn't my intention to add to that guilt. I've tried not to make *Celebrating Christmas As If It Matters* a finger-pointing book. There are enough fingers, including our own, pointed at us parents at this time of year. I've tried instead to create a book that fosters hope—and perhaps even enthusiasm, a book that makes you look forward to Christmas so that you can try some of these ideas. If I've been successful in that, I've done a good thing.

Thanks are due to many people:

To those dozens who consented to be interviewed for this book, sharing the successes and failures of their family Christmases. I found many families who've quietly, without fanfare, insisted on celebrating Christmas as if it matters, despite the strong pressure from our culture to be simply consumers.

To my editors, Sandy Vander Zicht, Lori Walburg, and Evelyn Bence. Every good book is a partnership between author and editor.

To Wayne Rice and Tim McLaughlin, editors of

Youthworker Update: The Newsletter for Christian Youth Workers, and to Youth Specialties, the publisher. *Update* is a great summary of current research and information about youth culture and family life; it saves hours of digging in primary sources, many of which I'd never have found anyway.

To Cindy, my wife, and to our kids: Sarai, Bryan, and Eric, who live with us all the time, and Seth, Anna, and Bethie, who live with us only sometimes. Our poor household endured countless hours of fatherlessness as I hid myself away with my Macintosh and a mountain of notes, books, cassette tapes, and magazine articles, but everyone still managed to maintain some enthusiasm for the project. (Partly because, as the younger ones still believe, this book is going to make me famous and all of us rich. We'll let them live in that fantasy world awhile longer.)

To my parents, who gave me a great model of how a supportive, loving, Christian family should operate—a model I had in mind throughout the writing of this book.

And to the Savior whose birthday we celebrate with joy and whose sacrificial love for us on a darker day makes that joy possible.

Chapter One

Why Christmas Matters

ACK ACK ACK ACK ACK! It was a plastic submachine gun, blasting my ribs. Son number three yelled, "Dad! We can get one of these for Craig, and I want one too! Just like this one!"

Guns for Christmas?

"Dad!" Son number two, waving a large box, came dodging through an incredible traffic jam of shopping carts piloted by unhappy, irritable parents. "Dad! This is the remote-control car I've been wanting!"

"But remember, we're here to choose presents for your friends, not for—"

"But this is the one I want! I just forgot to put it on my list. Can't you add it?"

"Bryan, look!" And the boys charged on to the next aisle—lined with action figures complete with weapons and attack helicopters—leaving me to mull over my misgivings. *Violent toys at Christmas. Isn't something wrong here?*

And then I looked more closely at the dozens of other parents—maybe you were one of them—jockeying their shopping carts past the Barbie dolls and the Teenage Mutant Ninja Turtles hardware and other ecologically disastrous plastic trinkets. I saw exhaustion and helplessness stamped all over these parents' faces, their carts full of senseless, overpriced toys they couldn't afford (as mine was), and I thought, *We're trapped in this thing. We don't like it, but we're trapped.*

Trapped—in a web of unnecessary Christmas activity, unfruitful Christmas spending, and Christmas guilt. Guilt that we're not celebrating Christ's birthday as he would like, that we're not making good use of our time and money, that we're not teaching our children proper attitudes toward Christ and toward possessions.

WHO DEFINES CHRISTMAS?

Christmas is meant to be a feast, a glad, cosmic cry of thanks to God, a generous sharing with those around us of our abundance, a time to give gifts and to receive them with thanks. This should hardly need to be stated—and yet it does, because most families have lost, in large part, the spirit of rejoicing and worship that should characterize Christmas for all of us. For many parents Christmas is no longer a celebration; it's a dreaded obligation.

How glad are we during those last days of hurried shopping, fighting crowds and traffic, finding that many of the stores are already out of the item we're seeking, trying to get packages wrapped and mailed in time to arrive by the twenty-fifth, and feeling angry with ourselves when it becomes obvious that we've failed? We're harried, irritable, and suffering from guilt. We're glad only when it's over.

Of course we rationalize our frustration and lack of joy by saying, "Well, Christmas is for the kids anyway— and they'll enjoy everything we're getting for them." Christmas is a good season for kids; that's true. Probably their favorite time of the year. But how often have you observed your children overanxious and irritable during the last days before Christmas and even on the day itself, disappointed with the toys they got and at loose ends when the orgy of wrapping paper and ribbon is over and when, by midafternoon, the cheaper toys have already broken?

Not to downplay the excitement of Christmas for kids. But can we honestly say that our children are getting from this most holy of seasons what they need? And I'm not talking about their wish lists; I'm talking about an understanding of the great gift God gave all of us on that first Christmas. I'm talking, too, about an opportunity to worship comfortably at home, to celebrate in a casual atmosphere (unlike that of church services, which most kids find boring and alien), to experience firsthand the strength of our personal relationship with God.

John MacArthur, Jr. states it well in his book *God with Us:*

> What concerns me most is that the spiritual values of Christmas are giving way to crass consumerism. Christmas has become the ultimate holiday for committed hedonists. Drunken parties, self-indulgence, madcap spending, and obscene gluttony all characterize the way much of the world celebrates Christmas. . . .
>
> The trends are not hard to document. Visit your local shopping mall during the week before Christmas, and you'll witness graphic evidence of how Christmas is rapidly slipping away from us. Notice how stores advertise their merchandise—and notice what they advertise. Listen to the shoppers talk. Stop by a card store and look at the greeting cards. Try to imagine that you are someone who has never heard of Christ or Christmas. What message would you get from what you see?
>
> More important, what does our Lord think of all this? That question continually weighs on me. Can we rationalize all this self-indulgent excess by calling it a celebration of His birth—He whose cradle was only an animal's feeding trough?[1]

Unfortunately, our society has recast Christmas in its own image, and there is no place in that image for the Christ whose birthday we're supposed to be celebrating. All those "Keep Christ in Christmas" bumper stickers didn't work; Christmas is now a retail event, a consumer holiday rather than a religious one. It's a great time of year to own a liquor store.

If there are a few "religious" TV specials this season, it will be because advertisers know that they'll draw a significant audience to sell their wares to.

Where is Christ in all this? Not in the public schools. In a typical case in 1987, the Fairbanks, Alaska, North Star Borough school district prohibited high-school students from posting the word *Christmas* on signs, posters, and bulletin boards. Students and teachers both were encouraged to substitute "Happy Holidays" for "Merry Christmas." "Student-council members put up a poster showing a person hanging from a noose. The caption read, 'But all I said was Merry _____.'"[2]

Nor is Christ likely to be found in any other public buildings. In a landmark 1980 case in Sioux Falls, South Dakota, the court established three standards for holiday observances in public buildings: "secular purpose, no primary effect of advancing religion, and no excessive entanglement between church and state."[3] Pretty hard to justify a manger scene by those criteria.

What does all of this mean? It means we celebrate Christmas as if Christ doesn't matter. As if nothing he said makes any difference anymore. As if we were ashamed of him.

We celebrate Christmas as if Christ were dead.

ONE FAMILY AT A TIME

It isn't this way because we Christians want it this way. We just don't know how to *change* it. I offer this suggestion: We change it one family at a time. This year, I can start with mine. And you can start with yours.

And what better place to start? In our frenetic, pluralistic society, most Christian parents have to *look* for ways to communicate their faith to their children. Not many families have regular family devotional times any more; some families are lucky to find one meal a week when they all sit down to the table at the same time. Many of us fortunate enough to look back on our own childhoods and see the many ways that our parents' Christian faith pervaded our homes look at our own children with grave concern: Are they "catching" our Christianity?

There is good reason for our concern, good reason for our despair over the eroding moral standards of secular music, movies, and television; about the violence, the drugs, and the rampant sensuality on our kids' school campuses and in our neighborhoods; about galloping materialism; about the attempts coming from all sides to subvert our efforts to raise our children as we believe they should be raised.

In the face of the magnitude of the forces against us and our children's attachment to those forces, we despair. So much of it is beyond our control! *We can do nothing about it,* we think.

But we *can* do something about it. We, as parents, can determine how our families celebrate Christmas.

Two years ago I sat with a group of parents lamenting the lack of time for family devotions, the difficulties of having devotions with kids who're bored by them because they're more used to the manic rhythms of the entertainment media. But we did more than lament. We brain-stormed ways of combating those difficulties, of fighting for the spiritual lives of our children. And of the dozen or so items on our action plan, this one was near the top of the list: *Communicate your faith to your children by the way your family celebrates sacred holidays.*

Is Christmas nothing more than an excuse to spend a lot of money, a hectic round of activities that leaves us exhausted and short-tempered? Do we permit retailers, advertising agencies, and the television networks to define Christmas for us? That communicates something to our children.

Or is Christmas a feast of joy and love? If we are conscious during this happy time of the Christ who was born out of love for us, if the ways we spend our time and our money are in keeping with our faith, if we are sharing love rather than gathering possessions—this, too, com-municates.

"As for me and my household," we can say with Joshua, "we will serve the Lord" (Josh. 24:15).

"What agreement is there between the temple of God and idols? . . . 'Therefore come out from them and be separate,' says the Lord" (2 Cor. 6:16–17). But in most of our families the evidence of that separation is difficult to see. Where should it be more evident than in the way we celebrate the birth of the One we serve, the One whose life and principles were so different from the world around him that society could not bear to see him live?

"O come, let us adore him," we sing. And in that adoration, we will separate ourselves from the Christmas

17

"idols" of the world: greed, excess, and self-indulgence. And Christ will be honored.

CHRISTMAS IS A ROOSTER CROWING

Besides helping us communicate our faith to our children, holiday celebrations serve another purpose in our families, one that may surprise evangelicals who pride themselves on being free from meaningless ritual: Holidays help satisfy the need and hunger children (and all of us, for that matter) have for ritual and tradition to give shape and meaning to the chaos that surrounds us.

In his fantasy novel *The Book of the Dun Cow,* Walter Wangerin describes a rooster, Chauntecleer, who leads all the other animals in the barnyard world they inhabit, even those much larger and stronger than he. Why is he their leader? Because he, by crowing several times a day to mark the passage of time and tell the animals when it is time for them to perform certain activities, gives their lives shape. When he is sick or discouraged and does not crow, the animals lose track of time, don't know what to do when, forget to do important things, and begin to panic. His crows

> told all the world—at least that section of the world over which he was Lord—what time it was, and they blessed the moment in the ears of the hearer. By what blessing? By making the day, and that moment of the day, familiar; by giving it direction and meaning and a proper soul. For the creatures expected his canonical crows, and were put at peace when

they heard them. "Yes, yes," they would say, "the day is our day, because Chauntecleer has made it ours." That they would say in the morning, grateful that by his crow the day should hold no strangeness or fear for them. And at noon: "The day's halfways over; the best part is still coming." It was a comfort to be able to measure the day and the work in it.[4]

As a child my world was circumscribed by traditions involving family. On Christmas Eve we went to my paternal grandparents' house for a gift exchange. On Christmas morning, home with my parents and brothers. Christmas afternoon, my maternal grandparents. On the Fourth of July, my church had a big picnic. Thanksgiving, summer, birthdays—throughout the year, there were certain "rooster crows" I could count on. I may have complained about them as a teenager, but even if I tried to skip them, I'd have been upset if they hadn't gone on without me. They gave my world shape and stability. They told me, as effectively as the period at the end of this sentence, that one section of time was ending and another beginning. They comforted me.

Times have changed. My generation chose to move away from home; of the cousins I played with at those family get-togethers, few stayed within driving distance of their parents. We followed our priorities: schooling, jobs, upward mobility. And because of those self-centered priorities, our marriages became notoriously unstable. But do our children, now so far separated from grandparents and extended family and even in many cases parents, have any less need for family tradition and shape-giving ritual than my generation did as we were growing up?

The answer is no. In *Power of the Family: Strength, Comfort, and Healing,* Paul Pearsall, professor at Henry Ford College, comments on one of the more alarming effects of lack of family ritual:

> Boys in gangs almost never have had a family ritual system in the home, and the gang's own rituals became substitutes, filling, at least temporarily, the individual gang member's needs for predictability and control. . . . Ritual within the family is one of the most important aspects of sound human development, physically, mentally, emotionally, and spiritually.
>
> Drug use, alcoholism, and the sometimes general disregard for the value of life shown by the senseless risks our young people occasionally take may be a symptom of lack of . . . consistency of family ritual. . . . All of adolescence in the United States may be seen as a mass cultural ritual evolving to fill the void of intimate family rituals.[5]

Similar observations have been made about the appeal of cults, satanism, and the occult to young people. Our children, like the barnyard animals in Wangerin's book, need "rooster crows"—events, activities, even sounds and tastes and fragrances that punctuate and give shape and meaning to their lives. And if our families and churches don't provide them, our children—and the industries that grow rich by raking off some of the eighty billion dollars American teenagers spend annually—will provide dangerous substitutes.

But our families don't have to settle for that. The taste of pumpkin pie can be a rooster crow. Singing

Christmas carols around a tree can be a rooster crow. Caroling at old folks' homes, sitting around a table as a family to sign and address Christmas cards—these and other holiday activities can not only teach our children our faith and "infect" them with our beliefs, but also answer their psychological need for structure.

Christmas is more than a dreaded responsibility—or a fun holiday. It is a celebration of our Lord's birth. It is a rooster crowing that another year has come around again, and that all is still well.

It is our chance, as parents, to offer our children a socializing factor of our own that is as attractive to them as television. And as compelling. It is their favorite time of year—and we, as parents, can control it. To their *benefit,* rather than to their detriment.

Christmas matters. Explore with me now some ways to celebrate Christmas as if we believed that.

Chapter Two

The Spirit of
Christmas Present

YOU BOUGHT THIS BOOK because you're dissatisfied with the way the birth of Christ is celebrated in our society. For yourself and your family, you want something better. That's the first step. But the next step is harder: How, then, *shall* we celebrate Christmas? If we could reshape Christmas (and we can) in a way that would be pleasing to God, what shape should it take?

The answer to that question has two parts: First, we need to identify precisely which elements in the modern, commercial Christmas we wish to avoid; second, we need to decide what to add in their place. In this chapter we'll address two items on the menu society offers us at

Christmas that we should steadfastly refuse: materialism and violence. In chapter 3 we'll address the celebratory elements that can fill any remaining void.

A NONMATERIALISTIC CHRISTMAS

A Christ-centered Christmas should emphasize the *spiritual* over the *material*. Why? Because possessions are wrong? No. Because Jesus said, "Be on your guard against all kinds of greed; a man's life does not consist in the abundance of his possessions" (Luke 12:15). And because emphasizing the acquisition of new possessions obscures the spiritual reality of Christ's birth.

Kenneth Kantzer, former editor of *Christianity Today,* chancellor at Trinity Evangelical Divinity Seminary, and a spokesman for evangelical Christianity, wrote in 1990:

> Not long ago I was invited to speak at a retreat for evangelical university students. They asked me: What is the greatest problem facing the church today? Without any hesitation I answered: . . . It is not liberalism or neo-orthodoxy or wrong views of revelation or inspiration or other controversial points in theology. . . .
>
> The most serious problem facing today's church is materialism—materialism not as a philosophical theory, but as a way of life.[1]

Why is materialism such a serious problem—more serious than liberalism, wrong views of inspiration, and other "heresies" that have mobilized strong opposition in evangelicalism? John Kavanaugh, a priest, has suggested an answer:

> In an economic system founded upon continually expanding consumption, in a society that already has a surfeit of goods, in a culture whose people are already overconsuming, what kind of person will best fit? . . . Is it better to have people with stable and happy lives or unstable and unsatisfied lives? Is it better for them to have a sound personal identity and fulfilling relationships, or to experience a personal and relational emptiness that must be filled in some way?
>
> The preponderance of programming and advertising in the U.S. delivers a continual message to the viewer: Human beings in relationship to each other are trivialized and alienated. People are most likely to be unfulfilled, unfaithful, unhappy, frustrated, foolish. The only times that persons are presented as uniformly happy and fulfilled are in commercials: purchasing, collecting or consuming products that resolve problems, deliver self-assurance, win friends.[2]

In short, materialism in our consumer-driven society encourages the exact opposite of the Gospel message and produces the exact opposite of the Christian character encouraged by Scripture. Few people can say with Paul, "I have learned to be content whatever the circumstances. I know what it is to be in need, and I know what it is to have plenty. I have learned the secret of being content in any and every situation, whether well fed or hungry, whether living in plenty or in want" (Phil. 4:11–12). Instead, materialism encourages people to be fulfilled and happy only when they are acquiring. Instead of people who find fulfillment through service to others and to God, materialism encourages people who find fulfillment "purchasing, collecting or consuming products."

Is materialism affecting the children we love and want to see embrace Christianity? Silly question—just look at where they hang out: shopping malls. "It's not hard to find evidence of why many specialists are now saying that today's teens are more materialistic, less realistic, and harder to motivate than any generation before them," wrote Jeffrey Zaslow in the *Wall Street Journal*.[3] He speculated that they visit malls partly out of an attempt to find values and structure lacking at home. Care to speculate about what values they're gaining when surrounded by thirty-seven clothing stores, eighteen restaurants, nine tape and CD shops, and Frederick's of Hollywood?

"Parents who do not spend time with their children often spend money instead," *Time* reported, and continued:

> "We supply kids with things in the absence of family," says Barbara MacPhee, a school administrator in New Orleans. "We used to build dreams for them, but now we buy them Nintendo toys and Reebok sneakers." In the absence of parental guidance and affirmation, children are left to soak in whatever example their environment sets. A childhood spent in a shopping mall raises consumerism to a varsity sport; time spent in front of a television

requires no more imagination than it takes to change channels.[4]

If Christmas is to be a celebration of God's redemptive gift, it should not also be a means of encouraging the "most serious problem facing today's church." But is a nonmaterialistic Christmas even possible, with the ever-increasing commercialism of that season surrounding us well before Thanksgiving? With each of our children now bringing us wish lists including several hundred dollars' worth of well-advertised, overpriced products they "really need"? Yes, but it isn't easy, and it takes preparation. And it's necessary.

Does it mean no gifts, no toys? No. Remember, this is a feast, a celebration, a time for rejoicing, a time for expressing our love for each other by the exchange of gifts, just as God the Father expressed his love for us on that first Christmas through the unfathomable gift of his own Son. I would be a grinch indeed to suggest eliminating the anticipation and excitement of Christmas morning's under-the-tree surprises.

But in recent years haven't we gone overboard? Isn't the amount we spend and the amount of time (especially last-minute time) it takes to buy and wrap all of those unnecessary gifts all but destroying the joy of the holiday season for the parents? Aren't many of the gifts themselves merely high-priced, low-quality, overadvertised junk that's just going to break or be forgotten by the next day? Of course, and we know it even as we write out the check.

If we want to celebrate the joy of the holiday season

27

as if it matters, we'll spend less on gifts and choose them more appropriately.

Will our children be disappointed? Not if we choose carefully, and especially not if in this season we give our children the superior gift of a greater amount of our time. The purpose of changing your family's Christmas traditions is not to make the season less enjoyable to your children—just the opposite. Each child can unwrap presents that he or she wants and enjoys. But this year let your children also find something different: opportunities to share your family's joy with others and an awareness of the living presence of the One whose birthday we celebrate.

A NONVIOLENT CHRISTMAS

You're probably reading this chapter in the fall or winter, but I'm writing it on the fifth of July. Yesterday my family and I braved a crowd of 350,000 people to go downtown and see President and Mrs. Bush in our Fourth of July parade, complete with a nationally televised fireworks display and the U.S. Army band. After all, how often do most people get to see the president of the United States? But, as exciting as that was, others in the parade received just as much applause.

This is 1991, you see. A few weeks ago the troops returned home from Operation Desert Storm. Many of them were marching in that parade in their desert camouflage fatigues, and the crowd went crazy: "Job well done! Welcome home! We're proud of you!" And all of us meant it. The tanks and cannons rumbling among the troops drew wild applause. Four F-15s flew over at a strategic moment, just above the skyscrapers, to a screaming chorus of shouts and cheers.

Another group marched that day, a sizable contingent of "Americans for Peace," mostly mothers and children. You won't be surprised when I tell you that their group received the silent treatment, despite the fact that they carried American flags and signs stating, "Peace is patriotic, too."

But peace is a nebulous thing; it doesn't excite us as war and violence do. It doesn't *seem* patriotic. It doesn't make good television. All of us watched the Persian Gulf war on television—watched the night skies over Baghdad lit with antiaircraft fire ("triple-A"—we all learned the lingo, didn't we?). We watched the broken, twisted aftermath of Scud missile attacks; we heard Tom Brokaw and Dan Rather praising the pinpoint accuracy of our weaponry without a mention of the loss of human life that had apparently just taken place before our eyes.

And all of our children watched that footage, fascinated, as their parents were, by the drama of war, by Saddam getting his. (Although it wasn't Saddam whose body was bulldozed into a pit, doused in gasoline, and burned.) And all of our children watched the amazing technology of war—the missiles (called "Patriot") that proved so effective in defending against the enemy's attacks, for instance.

And so it probably shouldn't have surprised my wife and me to come home from work one day and find our two sons playing Top Gun on their Nintendo set. Excited by war and by the American heroes of war, so lavishly praised on TV, they had borrowed the game cartridge from a friend. "Wouldn't you consider that a violent game?" I asked.

Violence, you see, isn't encouraged in our house. And the Nintendo set especially, having been a Christmas present just a couple of months before, came with a Christmas proviso: No violent games. No shooting people.

"No," they replied, ever arguing.

"You're shooting," I observed.

"We're not shooting people," they explained. "We're only shooting down planes."

It was a pretty bloodless war, as the television presented it. We saw twisted metal, but we didn't see many twisted bodies. We saw little blood. Maybe our sons had a point. But the game came out of the Nintendo set.

Don't misunderstand me; this is not a political statement, and this is not a political book. I'm merely pointing out that we live in a violent society—not simply a society in which violence occurs, but a society in which violence is encouraged and praised. War is violent. Justified or not, in self-defense or not, war is violent. In the kingdom of heaven, the lion will lie down with the lamb. In this world, we arm them both.

Even in nonwar years, our society is violent. A 1990 report by the University of Pennsylvania pointed out that American children average 27.3 hours of TV watching per week—four hours a day, *excluding* video-game and VCR time—more time than they spend in any other nonschool activity except sleeping. And during that time, they watch 26.4 violent acts *per hour*—up from 18.6 acts per hour only three years ago.

"Young children clearly imitate what they see," reports Dr. Comstock of Syracuse University's Center for Research on Aggression, reminding me of my sons and Top Gun. He continues,

> They do so particularly when aggression is not punished or when objectives are accomplished through the use of violence. Violence on TV definitely causes increased levels of aggression in children. The evidence is strong that the traditional violent cartoon programs lead to a higher rate of hitting, fighting and name calling in children.[5]

Other studies indicate that children exposed to extensive amounts of violence on television lack the ability to solve problems creatively; they resort to violence.

If there is ever a time to resist that message of violence and send a message of peace on earth, good will toward men, that time is Christmas, the birth of the Prince of Peace. Let us celebrate his birth without glorifying violence, brutality, or the taking of life.

If you have children, especially young boys, that resolution may be easier said than carried out. They may ask for toy guns or other weapons, violence-related "action" play figures, and so on. Sales of violent toys jumped 700 percent from 1982 to 1989, according to the National Coalition of Television Violence. Five of the six top-selling toys in the United States in 1989 were war toys.

Teenagers may ask for albums or posters from rock groups whose music glorifies violence or sexual brutality or for videos of violent films. Whether you allow them to purchase these items at another time of year is another question, of course, but my point is this: If we're celebrating the birth of One who taught us to eschew violence and to love one another to the point of sacrificing our lives, we cannot appropriately honor him by exchanging gifts that promote violence, anger, or rebellion.

As important as it is to avoid at Christmas those things that don't honor Christ on his birthday, Christmas is a time for positives, not negatives—for yes, not for no. I've included this chapter because you can't turn *toward* something without turning away from something else. But if celebrating Christmas as if it matters means eliminating from your Christmas celebration some things that your kids have been looking forward to, don't simply leave a void. Don't let your Christmas celebration be ruled by negatives: *non*materialism, *non*violence. Replace those less desirable elements with the positives we'll discuss in chapter 3: compassion, worship, peace, generosity, fellowship. Reduce materialism so that you can exercise compassion. Eliminate violence so that you can worship more freely.

Chapter Three

A Biblical Christmas: Honoring the Party Child

IN O. HENRY'S FAMOUS SHORT STORY "The Gift of the Magi," Della and Jim Young, poor, hard-working newlyweds in early twentieth-century New York, want desperately to give each other worthy gifts for Christmas. But they have no money. They have, in fact, only two valued possessions: Della's glorious, knee-length hair and Jim's valuable heirloom watch.

But she makes the sacrifice: She sells her hair to a hair-goods shop to buy Jim a beautiful platinum watch chain.

Arriving home after work on Christmas Eve, Jim is shocked to find his wife's hair as short as a boy's, and

Della fears that he's angry. He explains by showing her the present he had bought for her: an expensive set of combs she had long coveted—useless now, of course, or at least until her hair grows out.

But that doesn't reduce her excitement about her gift for Jim, and to salvage the evening she brings it out:

> "Isn't it a dandy, Jim? I hunted all over town to find it. You'll have to look at the time a hundred times a day now. Give me your watch. I want to see how it looks on it."
>
> Instead of obeying, Jim tumbled down on the couch and put his hands under the back of his head and smiled.
>
> "Dell," said he, "let's put our Christmas presents away and keep 'em a while. They're too nice to use just at present. I sold the watch to get the money to buy your combs."[1]

And in the end, of course, they're happier and more in love than ever because of this demonstration of their selfless love for each other.

A beautiful story, full of wisdom and good wishes. But mistitled. "Gifts of Love" or something like it would have been more appropriate. What do the gifts of these two lovers have to do with the gifts the Magi gave to the infant Jesus? O. Henry, like generations of us, has missed the point about the Magi's gifts: They gave them to Christ. Not to each other.

Not that there's anything wrong with giving gifts to each other; actually, it's one of the healthiest things we do at Christmas, as long as the gifts are chosen and given in good heart, as Della's and Jim's were. And indeed, as I'll explain below, what Christ asks of us on his behalf is that we give ourselves and our goods to one another, generously, as unto him. We are serving him when we serve each other.

Nevertheless, our approach to Christmas is as if we went to a birthday party, gave gifts to all the partygoers except the birthday child, to whom we didn't even speak, and then played with everyone else but him. An odd birthday party.

In some ways, I think the most appropriate Christmas celebration is the "birthday party for Jesus" that some parents of young children and some children's ministry workers organize at Christmas (discussed further in chapter 8). But even if you aren't a Sunday school teacher or the parent of young children, you can still celebrate Christmas as if it were truly Jesus' birthday. Anyone can speak love to the "party child" at Christmas and make sure he doesn't get lost among all the wrapping paper and thrown out with the bows and ribbons.

WHAT KIND OF CAKE DOES JESUS LIKE?

What Christmas lessons can we learn from the simple, ungrudging, courteous honors we bestow on any five-year-old's birthday? How do we honor a birthday child? We give him a party, for one thing. We go to some trouble on her behalf—putting up decorations, blowing up balloons, baking a cake. We dress up to enhance the celebratory spirit. (That's why little girls have "party dresses.") We laugh and have a good time with the birthday child. We play games—and whose favorite games do we play? Who chooses the flavor of cake and ice cream? Who chooses the restaurant or the movie? The party child. When it's your birthday, we do what *you* want. We don't say, "No way. I hate that. Let's go bowling instead."

And shouldn't we be doing the same with Christ's birthday? How dishonoring to the One who has done so much for us—using the holidays as an excuse for excess and self-indulgence, in defiance of his example and of the gentle instructions he gave.

A Christmas celebration that honors the party child will avoid what Christ hates and emphasize what he loves. A Christmas celebration that honors the party child will be designed in obedience to him, in accordance with his stated wishes.

"If you love me, you will obey what I command," Jesus told his disciples (John 14:15). And what are we to obey?

> "'Love the Lord your God with all your heart and with all your soul and with all your mind.' This is the first and greatest commandment. And the second is like it: 'Love your neighbor as yourself.' All the Law and the Prophets hang on these two commandments." (Matt. 22:37–40)

The commandments Jesus gave are not those that require us to minister to him. They require us to minister to God and to others. By his example, Jesus taught unselfishness. And if we love him, we will obey those commandments and love God and our neighbor in celebration of Christ's birthday.

By serving those in need, we serve Jesus himself. By giving to those who have not, we give to him.

A COMPASSIONATE CHRISTMAS

"Simon son of John, do you truly love me?" the resurrected Christ asked Peter (John 21:15).

"Yes, Lord," Peter answered, "you know that I love you."

"Feed my lambs," Jesus told him. Unselfishly, like a parent seeking the welfare of a beloved child, Christ asks us to express our love for him by turning our effort and attention to the ones he loves. His little ones. His followers. The ones he died for. Do you love him? If you, like Peter, answer yes with some sense of guilt—not long before that conversation Peter had denied even knowing Christ three times—then remember that Christ is less concerned with your past than he is with your future. Less concerned with how you've already failed than he is with what you intend to do now.

Feed his lambs.

"Religion that God our Father accepts as pure and faultless is this: to look after orphans and widows in their distress and to keep oneself from being polluted by the world" (James 1:27). And Jesus said, "I tell you the truth, whatever you did for one of the least of these brothers of mine, you did for me" (Matt. 25:40). What wonderful opportunities Christmas provides for a family to seek out little brothers and sisters of Christ, people for whom Christ died—many of whom have not even heard the Good News—and share with them out of the family's comparative abundance. Chapter 8 suggests several ways to help those less fortunate than your family.

We tell our children that, as Jesus said, "It is more blessed to give than to receive" (Acts 20:35). Am I being cynical if I suggest that our children will not fully grasp the truth of that statement (nor will we) if our only act of Christmas giving is to exchange unneeded gifts among the members of our close circle? When I suggest that we spend less on gifts for family and friends this year, it is so we will be able to establish a new pattern: spend less on unnecessary gifts for those who have few needs and more on necessary gifts for those who have many. This is true religion.

Charitable giving, alas, is unpopular these days. Empty Tomb, Inc., after studying the giving records of thirty-one denominations, discovered that, although average income after taxes and inflation rose 31 percent between 1968 and 1985, giving to churches, per member, dropped almost 9 percent. Perhaps even more disturbing is the study by Independent Sector that revealed that nearly half of the money being given to charity comes from households earning less than thirty thousand dollars a year. Households earning from fifty thousand to one hundred thousand annually give an average of 1.5 percent of their incomes to charity, while households earning under ten thousand dollars give 2.8 percent. Remember when you used to say you'd give more to your church when you were earning a little more?

Despite the great need for compassionate giving toward strangers, a compassionate Christmas must start at home. Not long ago I attended a large youth conference at which hundreds made a first-time commitment to Christ. Duffy Robbins, popular author and youth speaker, challenged those new Christians on the last night of the conference: "It'll be a lot harder to be a Christian when you go home tomorrow than it is here at this conference where everybody's slapping you on the back and saying, 'Praise God!' Wait'll you get back to your little brother. Wait'll you get back to your parents telling you to do things you don't want to do and telling you you can't do things you want to. That's where things get tough. But if your Christianity doesn't work at home, it doesn't work anywhere. Christianity starts at home."

This Christmas, let your compassion start at home as well. Rather than the usual pattern of the holidays—increased tension and lessened patience as time grows short and long lists of responsibilities wear on you—let your family's relationships be governed by compassion and love. With God's help, exercise patience and support toward your spouse and your children.

WORSHIP: SOMETHING FOR THE PERSON WHO HAS EVERYTHING

How, then—if the party child wants our gifts to go not to himself but to his father and to the ones he loves—do we give *him* anything in celebration of his birth? What's a birthday party without gifts for the party child?

There are ways. We can offer everything we give to others to him first. It is indeed a gift to offer them first on the altar to him, and then to use them as he directs us. No new thought. But a thought that seldom comes to any of us in the frenetic, materialistic, secular atmosphere of a 1990s Christmas.

Another way: We can give some gifts directly to him, such as our obedience. Our devotion. Our time. Our thoughts and words. Our bodies. Our money. And our worship.

A. W. Tozer said that worship is the missing jewel of evangelicalism:

> The purpose of God in sending His Son to die and rise and live and be at the right hand of God the Father was that He might restore to us the missing jewel, the jewel of worship; that we might come back and learn to do again that which we were created to do in the first place—worship the Lord in the beauty of holiness, to spend our time in awesome wonder and adoration of God, . . . doing nothing except as an act of worship to Almighty God through His Son Jesus Christ. I say that the greatest tragedy in the world today is that God has made man in His image and made him to worship Him, made him to play the harp of worship before the face of God day and night, but he has failed God and dropped the harp. It lies voiceless at his feet.[2]

Tozer's lament is as true of our Christmas celebrations as it is of our church services. Although we disparage the loss of the true meaning of Christmas, most of us do little to counteract that loss in our own families.

What a sad omission and lost opportunity, as even children resistant to Sunday school or family devotions embrace Christmas in its every—including holy—aspect.

"I want to know Christ," we and our families should be able to say along with Paul (Phil. 3:10), but it takes more than "Keep Christ in Christmas" bumper stickers to accomplish that. It takes sensitive, deliberate, and prayerful family leadership.

Can we somehow restore to this most important day a sense of worship and wonder unrelated to acquisitiveness and excess? Are there ways to reclaim Christmas as a religious holiday? Yes—ways that some Christian families have found work just fine.

The most obvious and probably the most important is to set aside family time for a specific purpose: to acknowledge Christ's birth and communicate its importance to your children. As they light the new candle in their Advent wreath each week, Bob and Shelley Hudson spend time in prayer and meditation. The important thing is to *plan* a time and then follow through. With the busyness of the season, things we don't specifically plan don't get done.

Many families, including my own, build that worship time around their nativity set. That's a good idea, especially if you have young children, because it enables them to visualize the discussion of Christ's birth. Poet and editor Bob Hudson remembers: "Our parents were wise in letting us play with the set; my sister and I would act out the story we had just heard in church. It made a real impression on us both; we formed a strong attachment to that set. My sister has it now, and I've written a cycle of poems revolving around the pieces of the set and the symbolic meaning they had for me."

Regardless of when you choose to gather your family to worship Christ, remember to make it an enjoyable experience for your kids. Sing carols and dedication songs such as "I Have Decided to Follow Jesus." Read the Christmas story from Luke 2:1–20 and Matthew 2:1–12, plus other sections as you think appropriate.[3] In fact, no matter what format your family's Christmas worship time takes, make Bible reading a part of it. Don't miss this opportunity to demonstrate one more time to your children that what we know about God we know from his Word.

Make that Bible reading as vital and as interesting as you can. Make it live for your kids.[4] Ask questions: What sounds do you suppose the shepherds were hearing, waiting quietly on the hillside before the angels appeared? What sounds in the stable? What's your favorite word in this verse? Can you make up a poem using that word? What's the opposite of *afraid? Joy? Peace?*

Afterwards, pass out treats and play games, or watch a video of Christ's life, such as *Jesus* or *Jesus of Nazareth.* After all, you want your children to remember this experience fondly, rather than as just another church service.

Because Christmas *isn't* just another church service. It may, in fact, be as close as our society comes to experiencing, on a nearly universal scale, a taste of the joy of heaven. That may seem an overstatement, especially in light of the hassles, frustrations, pressures, and disappointments of a modern Christmas. And yet when else do

millions of people gather simultaneously at thousands of
locations in scores of countries to sing this witness in
dozens of languages?

> *Joy to the World!*
> *The Lord is come;*
> *Let earth receive her King;*
> *Let ev'ry heart prepare Him room,*
> *And heav'n and nature sing!*
>
> *He rules the world with truth and grace*
> *And makes the nations prove*
> *The glories of His righteousness,*
> *And wonders of His love.*

It's true, of course, that many of those singing don't
understand the theological and cosmological importance
of the words they mouth, and yet they sing, with at least
some dim notion of the One whose praise they sing.
When but at Christmas do many of the world's people
who otherwise seldom give him a thought actually think
of—and praise—Jesus Christ?

A few years ago I wrote a story about a young boy who
loses track of his little sister in a crowded shopping mall on
the Saturday before Christmas. Frantic, he rushes through
the mall searching for her, and finally, scanning the lower
level from the railing on the second level, he spots her
watching the Christmas pageant put on by a local church.
He watches, embarrassed, as she follows the shepherds up
the stairs to the manger and then kneels with them before
Christ. An old man and woman in the audience nearby,
touched by her expression of worship, kneel too.

And that narrator guy, it sounds like somebody cranked his volume up a bit—or is everything else just getting quieter? *"But who may abide the day of his coming? And who shall stand when he appeareth? For he is like a refiner's fire . . ."*

I never heard *that* in any Christmas play before. And for just a second or two nothing happens. Then—just what I all of a sudden knew was going to happen and what I hoped like heck wouldn't—I see a nun kneel down over here, and a few people over there, and now *everybody* goes down. I mean a *hundred,* maybe. All around the crazy stage. Except for a few who get out of there fast. And now everybody in the whole mall is paying attention. People even come out of stores to see what's going on. And all through the whole wide mall, on all three levels, hardly anybody's moving and there's almost no noise.

And I think, *How can so much change in a split second?* Less than a minute ago I was just embarrassed. Then I had butterflies. Now I'm getting the pants scared off me. And I'm feeling guilty, too, like I'm supposed to do something and I haven't done it yet. Kneel, or what?

It's really spooky. And everybody else feels it too, I can tell. This place is quiet, man. It's in the air, whatever it is. If you told me there was a real, honest-to-God angel on top of the big Christmas tree, I'd look to see, I swear I would.

No I wouldn't, on second thought. Remember that part in the ten commandments story where, before Moses goes up the mountain, the people tell him, "Don't let God talk to us or we'll die"? That's kind of how I feel. Because whatever's going on here—well, crumb, even the old pillar of fire wouldn't surprise me now. . . .

And then the narrator says, *"Wherefore, God also hath highly exalted him, and given him a name which is above every name, that at the name of Jesus every knee should bow, of things in heaven, and things on earth, and things under the earth, and that every tongue should confess that Jesus Christ is Lord."*[5]

Not something most of us see at Christmas. And yet what we do see is at least a step in the right direction. For a change, during this season, most of our society is at least vaguely aware of Christ as both a historical person and as a fit subject for worship. In your Christmas this year, push things a little further, like the little girl in the story: Kneel and worship him. Others, especially those in your family, will kneel with you.

BRINGING THE GIFTS TO THE MANGER

Our family brings these ideas together in a worshipful way at a Christmas Eve celebration, after whatever other Christmas Eve activities we participate in. We gather around the crèche that serves as our "family altar" during the Christmas season.

We sing Christmas carols. We sing worship songs. We read from the Bible the story of Christ's birth. And then, prayerfully but not necessarily solemnly—this is, after all, a celebration—we conduct our own little gift-giving ceremony for the one whose birthday it is. Each family member writes on a piece of paper what he or she will give to Christ this year. (Our children are old enough to write their own lists. Younger children may need your help.) The papers are then folded and placed, one at a time, at the feet of Christ beside (or in) the manger.

That gift might be a pledge of time given to some worthy cause; it might be an amount of money or some possession given to help some ministry; it might be a change in attitude. The identity of the gifts is not as important as the principle found in Revelation 5:12: "Worthy is the Lamb, who was slain, to receive power and wealth and wisdom and strength and honor and glory and praise!" By our simple, humble gifts, we turn the attention of our Christmas observance toward the One who is worthy to receive our devotion and our gifts.

But the gifts themselves should be important to us. They should represent effort or value on our part and be something we feel would please Christ. If you try this in your family, you might bring those papers out a few months after Christmas and redistribute them to the givers for each to check on his or her own progress.

THE LAUGHING JESUS

If there's a danger for most evangelicals in trying to reshape the family's Christmas celebration along more biblical lines, it's that we'll take the whole thing so seriously that we won't have or be any fun. We may sing "Joy to the World" and "We Wish You a Merry Christmas," but our faces will look more like "Let All

Mortal Flesh Keep Silence" and "Man of Sorrows." There's unlikely to be anything merry or joyful about it; we'll be concentrating too hard on our mission from God. Not at Christmas, please. If we're honoring the party child at his party, we won't do it with a long face. This is the time to relax, forget the agenda, and spread good will. Think about this story from Tony Campolo:

> When my son Bart was just a little guy, I took him to Disneyland. After a wonderfully exhausting day of frontier rides and space rides and jungle rides, I finally broke it to Bart that it was time to leave the Magic Kingdom. "Just one more ride on Space Mountain, Daddy," he begged. When I explained that we were out of time and money, he countered assuredly, "Jesus wants me to have one more ride."
>
> How had he come to this glorious revelation, I asked him.
>
> "Last Sunday when you were preaching," Bart replied, "you said that Jesus feels what we feel. You said that when we cry, he cries. Right?"
>
> I agreed that he had indeed gotten the message right.
>
> "Well," he went on, "doesn't it figure that if he feels what we feel, then when we're laughing and having a good time, he's enjoying himself too?"
>
> I had to agree with the logic of his argument.
>
> "Then," he said triumphantly, "I think Jesus would enjoy me having one more ride on Space Mountain."
>
> Not bad theology.[6]

Nor is it a bad approach to planning Christmas. Surely, one fine gift we can offer Jesus on his birthday is to try to make sure that this Christmas several of those for whom he died, young and old, family members and strangers, enjoy themselves in some meaningful, lasting way. After all, if the Bible is true, whatever we do for others, we do for him. It really *is* Jesus laughing as he goes around Space Mountain one more time. (He obviously wasn't enjoying himself much when my wife rode it, though. If Bart Campolo's theology is accurate, I think Jesus was terrified when my wife rode Space Mountain. I'm sure I heard him scream several times, and I think he almost threw up.)

Don't take your attempts to reshape Christmas so seriously that you forget to enjoy the season. Relax. Be a host; make sure everybody's having a good time. Smile. And have a good one, yourself.

It's a great way of saying "Happy birthday to you, Lord Jesus."

Chapter Four

And a Partridge in a Pear Tree: Choosing Gifts

Every year at Christmas, the buying frenzy gets worse. Have you ever noticed, for example, how much stuff is sold that nobody needs? It doesn't have any practical use. It just sits there, collecting dust.

Our society is literally filled with the unnecessary, the insignificant, and the meaningless. And people spend a fortune on that kind of junk for Christmas. Why? Often, it is the quickest and easiest way to complete an obligatory Christmas list. What meaning is there in that?[1]

—John MacArthur in *God with Us*

Christmas gift giving is an opportunity to express our love for our family members and friends and to celebrate the season. But it's a risky opportunity. All of us—especially children—can become so excited about new possessions that the gifts themselves become the whole point of the holiday. And we can easily fall into the consumers' Christmas trap: spending money we can't afford on gifts that mean nothing.

To avoid that trap, keep two principles in mind: (1) spend less on gifts and (2) choose gifts more appropriately.

SPENDING LESS AND ENJOYING IT MORE

Why spend less? Isn't generous giving a positive attribute at Christmas time? Yes. But much of what we spend is unfruitful because the gifts are chosen without much thought—often last-minute, desperation buys. Money wasted, basically. Most of us have limited budgets for Christmas; if we're to have funds available for new Christmas activities and for giving to others outside the family circle—as we'll discuss in chapters 7 and 8—we need to limit the amount we spend on those we consider "family."

And that won't be easy. I sat with a father the day after his teenage son had been killed in an automobile accident, listening as he gave voice to his grief. He found comfort in reminiscing about the good times, the pleasant memories—such as Christmas shopping. "I could never say no," he chuckled sadly. "The boys would give me long lists of things they wanted, and I'd always swear to myself and my wife that they wouldn't get everything on those lists, because they already had more than they needed. But then I'd find myself walking through the store throwing all of those things into the basket anyway, plus a lot more besides just because I thought they'd like them. And I wanted to see their faces on Christmas morning."

A comforting memory for that father. But his sons would have loved him no less if he'd bought less. And we face the same choice every Christmas. We can do the "natural" thing, the American thing: lavish expensive, unneeded gifts on our children, far more than we can afford. Or we can choose a more biblical option: generously giving our children gifts that bring them joy while contributing to their growth, and also reaching out with generosity and compassion, as a family, toward those less fortunate than we are.

Spending less on gifts isn't easy in a consumer-oriented society. Here are some practical ideas that are not only less expensive, but also more meaningful:

Coupons

"One thing we did a couple of years ago when we were destitute at Christmas was to give the kids coupons for things we knew they'd appreciate," says Mike Yaconelli, author and editor of *The Door.* "One coupon said, 'Good for stopping one lecture sometime when you think we're reacting unfairly to something you've done.' Another said, 'Good for a family trip to the movies when you think we're too busy and not paying enough attention to you.' Others were simple: 'Good for a free hug.' 'Good for a game of Monopoly on demand.'

"The kids thought it was great! That was a couple of years ago, and they've still got coupons they bring out from time to time."

Many families—including mine—have tried this approach and been pleased with the results. Kids get the message loud and clear: My parents love me enough to give me not only the time it took to write these coupons, but also the time it will take to redeem them.

One caution: Don't give the coupons unless you're willing to back them up. Promises tell kids one thing; broken promises tell them something quite different.

Coupons also make a great gift for kids to give their parents or siblings. Any nonmaterial gift can be given by a coupon—a week's dishwashing, a fishing weekend, a bedtime story, an evening helping with homework, a back rub, a promise not to call a brother by a hated nickname.

This approach can be used outside the family too. If friends are forever having to pass up social opportunities because of the lack of baby-sitters, for instance, what better gift than a half-dozen "free baby-sitting for the evening" coupons?

Messages

This might be the most important thing you do for your children, or your spouse, this Christmas. At Christmas we parents worry about what kind of message we're sending our kids by the way we celebrate, by the money we spend, by the frazzled emotions. This year stop to figure out exactly what message you *want* to send them, and send it.

Make a list of family members and close friends. Beside each name write the message you'd most like them to hear from you this year. Do you have a son who needs to hear how much you love him? A daughter who needs to know that, even though she's made some serious mistakes this year, you haven't given up on her? A daughter who considers herself worthless and unattractive, stupid—but who is precious to you? A son who seems to have too high an opinion of himself, who needs to learn to pay more attention to others? Play this old game: If I were about to die and could say only one thing to these people I love, what would it be?

Third column on your list: How will you communicate those messages? It might be with a simple gift that symbolizes what you're trying to say, along with a card on which you've simply and lovingly stated your message. It might be face to face. It might be by including that child in some of your own Christmas activities—shopping, wrapping, visiting institutions, caroling—and explaining why. It might be by giving that child extra privileges—or responsibilities—for the coming year, along with an explanation.

It's true that actions speak louder than words. But people need the words too. Don't just "act" and hope your message comes through. Articulate it, even if that's difficult for you. Don't let your embarrassment or uneasiness deny your children or spouse or friend the comfort and reassurance you can provide them. If you merely act and don't speak, they may misunderstand the message. If you merely speak and don't act, they may mistrust the message. Do both. Convey and confirm.

Freedom

One of the most difficult aspects of parenthood is balancing your children's need for supervision and guidance with their growing independence. Here's a suggestion from Alice Lawhead:

> Christmas can become a rite of passage when you give a gift of freedom and, consequently, responsibility to your child. Children and teenagers will appreciate such gifts as:
> ◇ An extended weekend curfew.
> ◇ No more bedtime. (Accompany this gift with a reliable alarm clock that the child can use to get himself up in the morning.)
> ◇ A set of keys to the family car and resultant privileges to use the car.
> ◇ A handful of "You can count on me" phone call coupons. Each coupon entitles your teenager to a no-questions-asked ride home when he or she gets in a tough situation. . . .
> Freedom gifts are sometimes very difficult to give, and equally hard to receive. When they are given formally, though, at Christmas, they tend to be respected and used wisely.[2]

Something of Your Own

The effective propaganda of our consumer-driven economy has led us to believe that gifts, to be meaningful and generous, must be newly purchased. Even handmade gifts can be suspect these days. Even so, why not give your friends—or even family members—something you own that they've always admired?

That fishing reel your brother has commented on each time he's used it. That rare John Coltrane album Frank envies. The travel iron the Smiths have borrowed three times in the past year. The fringed leather jacket from your college days that your son keeps asking for because he wants to dye it black. Reluctant to give those things up? That's understandable. But remember that the more important such a gift is to you, the more its recipient will appreciate it.

A Charitable Donation

Many people—especially those who are already dissatisfied with the too-often-meaningless gift exchanges of Christmas—will be overjoyed to find that, instead of wasting money on trinkets, you made charitable contributions in their names. But be sure to match such contributions with their personal concerns and interests. A member of the National Rifle Association is not going to be pleased that you've donated fifty dollars in his name to the Sierra Club.

Drawing Names

An old idea that has served many families well. When you don't have the money to buy a gift for each family member or relative, or when you choose to spend that money on others who need it more, drawing names among siblings or cousins works just fine. An added benefit: when you only have one gift to buy, you can pick something much nicer than when you have to apportion the same amount of money among five or six people.

Says author Evelyn Bence: "My family has done this for several generations. I'm one of seven children, and to my earliest memory, we drew names among ourselves, so each of us got one 'nice' gift from a sibling, and gave one also. The dollar limit or price range was set by our parents when we were young. We've long since grown up, but most of us still follow that tradition every year, and all the nieces and nephews do the same—give a gift to one cousin, receive a gift from one cousin. It's a great way to maintain family ties without breaking budgets. But be sure someone keeps a master list of matches; someone always forgets whose name they drew."

White Elephant Exchange

Gifts don't always have to be expensive to be fun— in fact, we're wise to teach our children that sometimes, the sillier and more useless, the more fun the gift can be. Here's another suggestion from Evelyn Bence: "All my siblings and our families try hard to get together to celebrate Christmas sometime between Christmas and New Year's. The highlight of the day has become a white-elephant exchange—a 'Chinese auction' where everyone draws a number, picks a gift, and then trades or 'steals' someone else's yard-sale-type treasure if they'd prefer it to their own. Even grade-school children really get into this. It's the laughter that's memorable—not the gifts."

CHOOSING MORE APPROPRIATE GIFTS

Especially if we're spending less on gifts this year, it's important to choose those gifts appropriately. And that's easier said than done. We don't get much help with that from our children, who clamor for one expensive, advertised gift after another. We don't get much help from a social order based on the maxim "Whoever dies with the most toys wins." And we don't get much practical help from our churches, which usually either look benignly on our materialistic culture as appropriately American or rail against it without providing alternative suggestions.

And the hectic holiday season doesn't usually allow much time for contemplating such philosophical questions. That's why I'd suggest thinking through the selection of gifts early in your Christmas preparations. Some of the gifts you'll choose, such as magazine subscriptions, need to be arranged for early.

How does one choose more appropriate gifts? These four principles may help: (1) Look beyond the Christmas lists. (2) Choose gifts that stimulate rather than entertain. (3) Choose gifts that provide opportunities or experiences instead of more possessions. (4) Choose gifts that emphasize the uniqueness of the recipient.

Look Beyond the Christmas Lists

Your children will undoubtedly present you with long wish lists—mostly toys, clothes, and new additions to their hobby collection. Some of the items on that list you'll no doubt want to buy or make for them. But most of those items will reflect the skill of advertisers more than your children's wants and needs.

In the rush and desperation of the weeks before Christmas, we parents too often grab those hand-lettered lists and race through the store crossing off items. Our intentions are honorable, but we're doing our children no favors.

Look beyond those Christmas lists. What are your children's needs? At the current stage of development for each child—physical, emotional, intellectual, and spiritual—is there something else that should be on the list?

The inevitable answer to that question will be yes. Make new lists of your own, incorporating the best items from your children's lists along with the gifts you've chosen based on these simple principles.

Will your kids be disappointed that you haven't done as you've done in the past and simply given them what they asked for? Maybe. But here's a suggestion from Fred Rogers—"Mister Rogers" to your kids who watch his show on TV—that might help soften that blow. If possible, give your child the number-one item on the list, the thing he or she most wants. Having received the biggie, your child may not much lament the rest. In the long run, of course, if you've chosen wisely, the other gifts you give will prove much more enjoyable to your children anyway.

Stimulate Rather Than Entertain

Not that there's anything wrong with being entertained sometimes. But our leisure-oriented society expects to be entertained, and the entertainment we expect is most often passive. How often in the course of a year do you suppose most parents hear, "Mom, Dad—I'm bored"?

I'm bored—the admission of a passive people who've forgotten how to entertain themselves, who expect someone else to do it for them. And lots of people make lots of money by doing just that, from television networks to toy manufacturers. But persons lucky enough to learn early that they can entertain themselves by creative or physical activity are not at the mercy of the entertainment industry—and they'll be healthier, wiser, and more productive as a result.

When my oldest son was small and his newborn sister was too young to provide him much company, he began to fall into the "I'm bored" syndrome. Parking him in front of the TV to get him out of my hair wasn't an option, since we didn't have a TV. (That came later.) So I stocked a low cabinet with art and craft supplies and then helped him make a long list of activities he could do on his own anytime he felt at loose ends. It didn't always work, because sometimes the problem wasn't really boredom but loneliness. He wanted my touch and my company. Still, the principle is sound: It's better (if not always easier) to stimulate a child's development than to tranquilize with mindless entertainment just to shut the child up.

Choose gifts that stimulate the intellect or the senses, that encourage creativity. Art or drawing supplies, musical instruments, additions to hobby collections, magazine subscriptions (for many years, my parents have given each of their children's families a subscription to *National Geographic),* books, and sports equipment are usually excellent choices.

Provide Opportunities or Experiences

Think in terms of providing opportunities rather than merely more possessions. Consider tickets to concerts or for bus or train rides to visit family or friends; memberships in hobby organizations or health clubs; gift certificates to restaurants or hotels. Commitments to participate in shared experiences (like family weekends away from home) do much more to enrich life than a new sweater or a new teapot.

Each year Cal and Mary Buist and their kids spend the weekend after Christmas at a motel with several branches of their extended family. "We don't exchange presents with them," Mary explains. "We discussed it and decided that we didn't want to end up doing each other's shopping. Instead, we wanted to spend time together."

A couple of months ago I needed to spend a few days in Washington, D.C., on business. I took two of my sons with me. Not a cheap trip, I assure you. But it was worth it for those boys to spend that time with me, to visit the Smithsonian, to walk through the Capitol, to stand in front of the White House, to shake hands with (and get autographs from) some of the Christian entertainers and speakers I was there to see. If you're aware of similar opportunities you can offer your children in the coming year, make that adventure a part of your Christmas gift to them.

You might even consider making sure that each family member gets, as part of their Christmas each year, a gift of time. Perhaps mom and dad get to plan a weekend away together as part of their Christmas gift to each other, and each child gets a coupon for a day's activity with one parent or both—a day's fishing trip for one child, a trip into Chicago shopping with mom for another, a weekend backpacking with dad for another, or maybe a ticket to see grandma down in Florida. These gifts of time aren't always inexpensive, but they'll certainly be remembered longer than most others.

Emphasize the Uniqueness of the Recipient

A special present can encourage personal interests or talents. The guitar my parents somehow managed to save enough to buy for me in sixth grade encouraged me to develop my musical abilities; I earned part of my way through college writing and performing music.

The Buists try to emphasize the individuality of their children both in the selection of the gifts and in how they're presented. "We try choosing one of each child's gifts to reflect that child's 'specialness'—the special gifts or talents or interests that God has given that child," Mary explains. "Then, just before we open our presents, we discuss, as a family, what unique and special qualities each family member has."

Choosing gifts that emphasize the uniqueness of the recipient takes some thought, of course. For instance, you can't simply buy a model car for each child in the family. If one child gets piano lessons, the next might get a baseball mitt. If one gets a cassette recorder, another might get a pocket calculator, and another might get a fishing pole. One gets a subscription to *Sports Illustrated for Kids;* one gets a collection of fairy tales; another a Bible.

How do you decide for each child? Start by asking these questions:

◊ What brings this child the most joy?
◊ What does this child absolutely hate?
◊ What does this child do surprisingly well?
◊ What is this child best at in school? Worst at?
◊ When this child disobeys and gets in trouble, what is it for?
◊ How is this child different from his brothers and sisters, or from other children his age?
◊ Based on her current interests, talents, and hobbies, what might you expect this child to be when she grows up?

Surprisingly, it's just as hard to pick gifts that emphasize the uniqueness of the adults on your list. The rabid sports fan on your list, for instance, may also like opera, but his buddies feed his sports interests, and for the sake of friendship and acceptance he keeps that interest in sports on the surface, easily visible. Who encourages his interest in opera?

Ask these questions:

◊ What do you know about this adult that would surprise someone who doesn't know her as well as you do?

◊ What is the difference between his public persona and his private self?

◊ If she hadn't chosen her particular career path, is there something else—perhaps something very different—that she might have been even more happy doing?

For both children and adults, it's helpful to do your gift planning *away* from stores and catalogs. Start with an awareness of the person you're buying for, and brainstorm types of gifts that suit that individual. When confronted with a cornucopia of merchandise in a store or catalog, it's too easy to choose something in front of you and think, *Well—close enough.*

Why is it so important to give gifts that celebrate our individuality? Because it's one way we Christians can combat society's pressures to conform to a mold that doesn't acknowledge the uniqueness of each individual as created by God.

> We were all baptized by one Spirit into one body. . . . If the whole body were an eye, where would the sense of hearing be? If the whole body were an ear, where would the sense of smell be? But in fact God has arranged the parts in the body, every one of them, just as he wanted them to be. If they were all one part, where would the body be? (1 Cor. 12:13, 17–19).

As a member of the body of Christ, each of us has a function to perform within that body. As we grow in Christian maturity and in our ability to perform our unique functions (as one of us becomes more like an eye, in other words, and another more like an ear), we will become less like each other in many ways. But society—even Christian society, unfortunately—doesn't encourage diversity. It encourages conformity. Sports over opera. The pragmatic over the visionary.

Let's not play into its scheme. Ask for God's guidance in sensing the uniqueness of the individuals on your shopping list, in distinguishing what gifts and talents God gave them that perhaps he didn't give you or anyone else you know. Then celebrate that uniqueness through your selection of gifts.

And may those gifts be like the gold, frankincense, and myrrh brought by the Magi—precious, and of a fragrance rare and pleasing to the birthday child.

Chapter Five

When Is Christmas?

CAL AND MARY BUIST AND THEIR FAMILY open their Christmas presents right after their big turkey dinner.

Right after their big Christmas turkey dinner? No—right after their big *Thanksgiving* turkey dinner.

"We started exchanging our gifts at Thanksgiving so we could focus our attention at Christmas on Christ's birth," says Mary. "All of our shopping and wrapping is done before Thanksgiving."

"The time we save at Christmas we spend in activities that center our attention on Christ—viewing some of the local 'live' nativity scenes, for instance. We started this system when our children were very young, and they have no desire to switch to a more conventional approach."

Does this deviation from the usual Christmas time-table cause the Buists any feelings of isolation? "We try not to alienate anyone—extended family members, for instance—by forcing them to comply with our calendar. If they want to send us their presents at Christmas rather than Thanksgiving, that's fine. And the time we gain at Christmas gives us *more* time, not less, to participate in Christmas activities with family and friends."

"We do our shopping by catalog," explains Wally Metts. "We have it all completed by the beginning of November. We give our kids the catalogs to look over; then we consider their preferences and order what we think is appropriate. Between Katie and me, we have twelve siblings, so we order gifts for them through the catalog, too. And often we order the same thing for all of them, sometimes as an expression of our commitment to compassion or social concern—last year it was a box of pencils from the Blackfeet Indian Reservation in Montana. We shop that way—and that early—for a couple of reasons: to avoid the crowded malls and stores during the Christmas rush, which we hate, and to have all of the shopping out of the way before Advent begins so that we can devote Advent to worship and to our family and to reaching out to others in some way other than with dollar bills."

"Every day of Advent," Joyce Rogers explains, "each member of our family would participate in some act of giving to someone else. Sometimes it would be in secret, such as an anonymous gift or a prayer for someone going through a hard time. Other times it would be openly, such as taking the time to write a letter to someone. The idea was to spread out the act of giving, to make it a daily activity during Advent, rather than a one-day event."

"Rather than a one-day event." But for most of us, Christmas *is* a one-day event. A boom followed by a bust to end all busts, emotionally and physically as well as financially. Oh, sure, there were weeks of preparation ahead of time, all that shopping and so on. But that was all just leading up to the main event: You wake up and it's the Big Day, and then you clean up the mess and it's all over, except for a week of turkey sandwiches and taking stuff back to the store to exchange.

Some families want it like that—stressful but exciting. For others, it's too much of a good thing. Overkill.

For those families, a far wiser, more effective, and in the long run more enjoyable approach would be to spread out the intensity of the holiday, to—like the Buists and the Mettses and the Rogerses—"spread out the act of giving," so that the holiday season would be filled with "activities that center our attention on Christ."

There are lots of ways to do that. The possibilities are limited only by your imagination. But in choosing a timetable for your Christmas season, remember the purposes:

1. To keep at least a part of your Christmas celebration free from the distraction of the acquisition of possessions, no matter how well-intentioned those gifts

might be, so that time, money, and energy can be spent on activities that express Christ's spirit.

2. To emphasize that, for Christians, giving is a way of life, not a one-day activity. By condensing the "giving" aspect of Christmas to one day, we distort and compress the giving concept and hide God's intention for our lives. We emphasize the "receiving" over the "giving" aspects of the holiday. Doesn't God intend us to give generously and selflessly year-round? "Just as you excel in everything—" Paul said to the Corinthians, "in faith, in speech, in knowledge, in complete earnestness and in your love for us—see that you also excel in this grace of giving" (2 Cor. 8:7). To rise from our current practices to achieve excellence in the "grace of giving" in one year might be too much to ask. But, just maybe, this year your family can get the idea that, instead of simply exhausting themselves with giving on one day, you're going to practice giving over a short period of time—Advent, perhaps, or Christmas week. That's a start. And within a period of a few years, perhaps you can lead your family into practicing an attitude of giving all year long.

3. To reduce stress, for yourself and for your family. Christmas should be a joy; by spacing out some of the activities of Christmas, you might be able to restore some of that joy.

4. To take greater advantage of the opportunities Christmas provides for passing along your faith to your children and strengthening in them the awareness of Christ.

The most creative and appropriate ways to accomplish those objectives for your family will probably be the ones you think up yourself. But, to start your brainstorming, here are some suggestions for avoiding the Christmas morning, under-the-tree orgy of gift-receiving and for "spreading out" your family's Christmas celebration both before and (don't panic—wait until you hear me out) even after Christmas.

HOW FAST CAN YOUR KIDS OPEN 176 PRESENTS?

Let's face it—some families don't *want* to avoid the gift-unwrapping orgy under the tree on Christmas morning. They enjoy it too much. They'd prefer to find other ways to accomplish the objectives listed above.

Other families are uncomfortable with that consumer's extravaganza and would like to find other patterns for exchanging gifts that don't so thoroughly distort and monopolize the holiday. Not all families can (or want to) switch their gift giving to Thanksgiving, as the Buists did. Here are some alternatives:

◇ You probably aren't giving a partridge in a pear tree, but handing out a present a day for twelve days isn't a bad idea. You might begin on Christmas Day with the "main" present for each family member, then follow on the remaining eleven days with more modest presents or presents from different members of the family. And just think—that means that your shopping doesn't *have* to be done by December 25! You can take advantage of the after-Christmas sales! (This approach can work during the Advent period too, by the way; in fact, it might be psychologically more satisfying, allowing you to build toward the "big" present on Christmas Day. If your family uses an Advent calendar, one option would be to distribute a present or express an appreciation to each family member each day when the new Advent calendar symbol is revealed. Or you could keep the "twelve days" approach, starting on December 14.)

◇ *The Alternate Celebrations Catalogue* reports that one doctor's family begins their gift opening on Christmas Eve morning with one present at a time—and continues opening through that day and the next at the rate of one present per person every four hours. The obvious advantage: Each gift is accorded real importance and is enjoyed and appreciated in itself for a period of time, rather than being dropped in someone's lap while the family rushes on to the next. The emphasis is on appreciation of the gift and the giver, rather than on acquiring more.

◇ Even if you decide against spacing the gift opening out that way, remember: Don't rush! Wait until each family member is ready for the next present before handing him or her another. Younger children, especially, enjoy proceeding at their own pace. If they open toys and want to play with them for a half-hour then and there, let them. Sit back; sip your coffee; relax—and take a moment to enjoy watching your kids at an age they'll never be again. Take a picture.

BEFORE AND AFTER

If you're interested in "spreading out" your Christmas, there are, obviously, two directions you can go. You can spread it out before Christmas Day. You can spread it out after Christmas Day. Or you can do both.

Advent

Not all Christians—especially Protestants from the more evangelical or fundamentalist ranks—respond positively to liturgical words like *Advent* and *Lent.* Baptists don't observe the church calendar. Do they?

No need for suspicions about the church calendar. Observances of traditional church holidays can be as meaningful or as meaningless as any individual church, or any individual Christian, chooses to make them.

There's nothing mysterious or mystical about Advent. It's simply a period of waiting for Christ's coming—or "advent." It commemorates the centuries God's people waited for the birth of the Messiah they had been promised, and it looks ahead to his Second Coming—Second Advent. The traditional season begins on the fourth Sunday before Christmas and ends on Christmas Eve—lasting about four weeks.

Even nonliturgical churches frequently nod their heads at Advent; our church, for instance, has an Advent wreath on the wall behind the pulpit, and the appropriate candle is lit during the Sunday morning worship service each of the four Sundays before Christmas.

Advent provides opportunities to enrich our Christmas experience. There is clearly a spiritual benefit in taking that time to prepare ourselves prayerfully to receive God's great gift and in reliving, at least symbolically, the agonizing centuries of waiting for the promised Messiah. There is also the chance to "spread out" some of the Christmas activities and experiences so that we lessen the chance of overkill on Christmas Eve and Christmas Day. Here are some creative suggestions for realizing those benefits:

◇ Ron and Joyce Rogers's idea of planning a special gift or act of giving for someone each day of Advent is one variation on a popular approach: participating, on each day of Advent, in some special Christmas activity—baking Christmas cookies, writing Christmas cards, reading a Christmas story, going caroling.

Many families already use Advent calendars—every day opening the appropriate door to find a surprise symbol or treat—or light candles on Advent wreaths. Many trim their trees around the beginning of Advent—not by design, perhaps, but because the kids can't be put off any longer. Shortly after Thanksgiving the boxes of trimmings come out and the pine-cone wreath goes up on the front door, the plastic Santa into the window, the crèche onto the coffee table.

It might be more effective, though, to approach Advent a little more formally. Place the crèche in its accustomed place on the Sunday that marks the beginning of Advent with a little family ceremony that includes songs and the initiation of the Advent calendar or wreath. And every day in Advent, let there be some activity that reminds all of your family what time of year it is, and what the true spirit of the holiday is.

◇ In *The Alternate Celebrations Catalogue* Jeann Schaller reports on a variation on the "Twelve Days of Christmas" theme that would take place during the Advent period:

> We have 12 candles on the fireplace mantle. We start lighting them on December [13] until all are lit on December 24. We sing carols and read Christmas poems and stories for the 10 to 15 minutes the candles burn.[1]

◇ One enjoyable and spiritually meaningful practice during Advent, especially for younger children, is to create a Jesse Tree—a tree decorated with symbols of Jesus' heritage: a Bethlehem skyline, a star of David, Jacob's ladder, a crown, Noah's ark, and so on—Jesus' "family tree." You can use your Christmas tree, mount a tree branch, or even create a tree out of construction paper or felt to hang on the wall. Think up your own symbols or use the patterns in *The Jesse Tree: A Cutout Book,* by Marlene Konrady (Winston

Press, 1984). Let your children help in making and hanging one new symbol a day (or every other day) during Advent. As you hang each, give a brief explanation of the symbol or read a short passage of Scripture concerning it. Explain how each event or person represented helped prepare for the coming of the Messiah.

An alternative to a Jesse Tree would be a Waiting Tree. Instead of symbols of Christ's heritage, use symbols of waiting—an acorn, an egg, a cocoon, a sunrise, a seed, a tadpole, and so on.

◇ If you've been able to keep your Advent period sufficiently free from the necessity of shopping and scrambling around making other last-minute preparations, you'll find more opportunities for socializing. "The first Sunday of Advent," explains Wally Metts, "we invite some of my students at Spring Arbor College; the second Sunday, someone else from the college—a colleague, maybe, but preferably one I don't know well. That second Sunday has been risky for us; we've invited deans, administrators—and we have a simple, country home outside of town, probably not the sort of place they're used to being invited to. The third Sunday of Advent, we invite someone from our church, perhaps an older couple. Again, we try to pick someone we don't know well. And the fourth Sunday, we invite a family who aren't practicing Christians.

"Typically, on those Sundays, we'll have

some simple food—a cheese ball, maybe. We might string popcorn and cranberries for the tree. We'll socialize; their kids will play with our kids. And then we have a simple service: We'll read a devotional, let someone choose a song for us all to sing. Then one of the kids will light the appropriate Advent candle in the wreath, and we'll sing a carol. And we always have a simple gift for everyone who comes—maybe something the kids have made, or sometimes it's been homemade jam or a Christmas ornament for each visiting child.

"That's it. It's a simple thing, but it's a way for our family to reach out with the love of Christ. And the kids look forward to it. They'll ask who's coming way ahead of time, and we involve them in the preparations."

◊ When your young children simply get too excited in their anticipation of Christmas and need diversion, divert them with Christmas crafts and games: making red and green hats and instruments out of construction paper for a Christmas parade; cutting and pasting old Christmas cards to make "new" cards for select family friends or to make gift tags; making name tags for the holiday dinner table; making Advent posters or mobiles composed of stars or snowflakes; or playing active games like Christmas charades. Books such as *Joyous Days: A Collection of Advent and Christmas Activities* by Sharon Lee contains scores of ideas such as these:

Christmas Cartoons

A cartoon is not necessarily always funny. A cartoon can be a story told in a series of pictures in boxed frames with dialogue in balloons pointing to the characters who are speaking. Having children make a cartoon is another way of illustrating the Christmas story.

Process:

◊ Decide how many frames (pictures) each cartoon will have, what each frame will show, and the words that will be in each frame.

◊ Draw each cartoon in its frame.

◊ Add words in a balloon.

Make a large cartoon on mural paper. Ask one [child] to be responsible for the development of each [section] of the cartoon.

Christmas List

Hand out pieces of paper with the word CHRISTMAS written across the top. Encourage the children to list as many words as they can think of using [some or all of] the letters in CHRISTMAS. A letter may be used twice in a word only if it appears twice (e.g. s). . . . Set a time limit, perhaps four minutes.

Christmas Peek

Arrange fifteen to twenty-five objects (ornament, ornament hanger, ribbon, gift wrap, star, straw, candle, angel figure, cookies, gift tag, candy cane, Christmas card) on a tray. Place a cloth or towel over the objects. Gather the children around the tray and remove the cloth. Give them one minute to carefully examine the objects. Cover the tray. Specify an amount of time and challenge the children to list as many objects as they can remember.

Christmas Stocking Race

Collect a basketful of large socks. Ask the children to take their shoes off and sit in a circle. Place the basket of socks in the center of the circle. Tell the children that they will wear blindfolds and race to see who can put on the most socks in two minutes. Blindfold the children and begin timing them.[2]

If yours is an only child, or if your children differ too widely in age to participate in many activities together, books such as *Fun Things for Kids at Christmastime,* by Sarah Liu and Mary Lou Vittitow (Standard Publishing, 1991) provide numerous activity sheets and pencil games suitable for younger children to use alone.

◇ Many families use their nativity set creatively during Advent to encourage a sense of Christ's imminent birth. Ron and Joyce Rogers set up their crèche early in Advent but don't put the figure of the infant Jesus into the set until Christmas Eve, to build anticipation for Christ's coming. Other families celebrate his arrival by following a Polish custom: setting a tiny ladder near the crèche and bringing the infant Christ down the ladder rung by rung, slowly, throughout

Advent. Another family builds anticipation and symbolizes Christ's coming "for all" by moving the figure of the infant Jesus through each of the rooms of the house during Advent, finally placing him in the manger on Christmas Eve.

These families have found ways, for their own benefit, to break a destructive pattern. Follow their example. Each of our families, this year, can try to free Christmas Day from the tyranny of gimme gimme gimme.

The Twelve Days of Christmas

If you can't get yourself into gear early enough to begin your Christmas celebration during Advent—no problem. Sounds like the twelve days of Christmas is custom-made for you.

Remember the song "The Twelve Days of Christmas"? The twelve days it talks about are the twelve days beginning on December 25 and ending January 5, sometimes called Twelfth Night. Then January 6 is Epiphany—the day the church traditionally has celebrated the visit of the Magi to the infant Jesus—even though, in all likelihood, the Wise Men visited Mary and Joseph and the Christ child about two years, not two weeks, after his birth.

Before you scream in anguish, throw this book across the room, and yell, "Never! By December 25, I'm through with Christmas! I have no interest in dragging it out for twelve more days!" consider the stress relief those extra twelve days might provide. For instance:

◇ Feel guilty every year because you have a hard time getting thank-you cards written and because you're not teaching your kids to write them? Make it a family activity during the twelve days of Christmas.

◇ If getting Christmas cards out in time for Christmas every year is just too much for you, stop trying. Why accept that much stress every year when you have an after-Christmas period perfect for writing cards—and even letters to go in them if you like. Besides, this way you don't have to worry about forgetting anyone who might send you a card; you already *know* who sent you cards.

◇ As a way of exercising generosity and compassion and teaching your children the importance of giving rather than simply receiving, let your children know before the presents are opened that each member of the family will be choosing (if he or she agrees) two gifts from the Christmas bounty to give away to someone else who probably didn't receive such fine gifts. Then, in the days following Christmas, take those new toys or clothes (along with anything else your family would care to share—for instance, canned goods or other clothes or toys or books) as a family project to a needy family, group home, hospital, or orphanage. (One caution regarding this idea: If the feelings of gift-givers are likely to be hurt—in other words, if Jack is likely to be upset that Jill chose to give away the gift *he* bought for her— then it's better to restructure this activity to include only used clothes, canned goods, and perhaps some things your family will choose to buy for the other family.)

◊ Here are some additional ideas from Alice Slaikeu Lawhead's *The Christmas Book:*

> After Christmas, decorate an outdoor tree with popcorn or bread cubes on string or homemade suet balls as a gift to the birds and wildlife. Maintain the tree throughout the winter.
>
> . . . Save all your entertaining for after Christmas. Enjoy attending the church and social functions to which you are invited before Christmas, and do your own parties after.
>
> . . . Plan a big project that will last throughout Epiphany. You could work on a family cookbook. . . . Sort through the year's snapshots. . . . Build a birdhouse or feeder. . . . Pace yourself so the project will be completed on January 6. Plan some ceremony to mark its completion.
>
> . . . It has been traditional to remove all holiday greenery from the home and burn it on January 5. Depending on where you live, and the codes regulating open fires, you might make a custom of having a bonfire fueled by Christmas garlands and trees—your own and your neighbors'.[3]

One suggestion: If you plan to include the "twelve days" in your Christmas plans this year, and you don't want to be accused by your family of being a procrastinator (even if it's true, and so what if it is?), you might want to offer some explanation well ahead of time: "You've heard of the twelve days of Christmas? Well, they start on Christmas Day and last until a celebration sometimes called Epiphany, on January 6. This year, we're going to do some of our Christmas activities during that time. It'll be fun! It'll make Christmas last longer!"

The Day After Christmas

In the United States, the day after Christmas has become a day to return to the stores all the gifts that didn't fit or were broken or unwanted. In Great Britain, Canada, and Australia, December 26 is called Boxing Day. If you're like me, you've often wondered, when British friends mentioned this holiday, why otherwise civilized people would make a national holiday in honor of such a brutal sport. Shows how much we Yanks know.

The name "Boxing" dates from the Middle Ages when it was customary to open the church "poor box" on this day and share the money among the poor. Another "Boxing" custom was presenting money as a gift, in a small box, to those who had given service during the year, such as the postman, the milkman and the servants.

In modern Boxing Day observances, many families attend theatres and modern versions of the age-old "Christmas Pantomimes," in which traditional stories are mixed with dancing and light-hearted fun. Sports and outdoor activities are a welcome change after the heavy eating and celebrations of Christmas. City parks are crowded with children and their model aeroplanes, roller skates and bicycles. In Canada and wherever there is plenty of snow, sledding, building snowmen and snowball contests are a common sight. In Australia, where the season is summer, swimming, surfing, and yacht-racing mark Boxing Day.[4]

Susan Schaeffer Macaulay, daughter of Edith and Frances Schaeffer, remembers Boxing Day activities from her childhood and keeps those traditions alive in her own family now:

We . . . keep the wonderful English tradition called Boxing Day, on December 26. That morning we would choose one parcel from one of the relatives we've been separated from, and we'd sit on the bed and [open the parcel together]. Sometimes we've opened our presents over a whole week—one day we'd open my sister's parcel, another day, my brother's, and so forth, so the children wouldn't be confused as to what they'd received from whom. We felt the children appreciated each one more that way. They'd say, "Oh, yes, this is what _____ planned for me."[5]

December 26 is also St. Stephen's Day, or the Feast of Stephen, named for the first Christian martyr, who calmly submitted to execution rather than deny his belief in Christ. His feast day was set on December 26, the day after Christmas, as a special honor.

Whether you think of December 26 as Boxing Day or the Feast of Stephen, it's a perfect day either for expressions of your family's compassion or for outdoor family activities. And best of all, it provides one more way in which you can delay some of the Christmas activities until after Christmas.

Don't be a slave to traditional Christmas timetables this year. Let your family find its own pace. You may find that much of the stress you've been experiencing every year has been simply a matter of timing.

Chapter Six

Thanks for the Memories

CLOSE YOUR EYES. Think back to the Christmases of your childhood.

What do you remember? Family activities, probably—things you did with your parents and brothers and sisters, as well as grandparents, cousins, uncles, and aunts. Christmas caroling on frosty evenings. Getting hoarse from singing so loudly in the cold. Snow down the back of your neck while out sledding or tubing. Wearing your bathrobe in the Sunday school Christmas program, pretending to be a shepherd.

Oh, and the aromas of that family Christmas dinner!

CELEBRATING CHRISTMAS AS IF IT MATTERS

The taste of pumpkin pie with whipping cream, cranberry sauce, cider, mashed potatoes with turkey gravy.

The things we remember are the things we experienced either with our senses—the things we felt, smelled, tasted, heard, or saw—or through active participation (such as caroling or sledding or acting in the church Christmas program).

Here's a childhood Christmas Eve memory from Katrine Stewart, daughter of authors Walter and Ingrid Trobisch; notice how full it is of sensory and participatory touchstones:

> We would have a simple meal, usually sausages and potato salad. (Don't ask me why.) After cleaning up, we would all walk into the living room and help light the tree candles. (This was also the only evening of the year when we burned incense. They smoldered inside a little carved mountain dwarf and pipe smoke came out of his mouth.) Then Father began to act as master of ceremonies for our family Christmas program. The program had already been planned and prepared weeks earlier. *Every* family member and guest was expected to contribute an instrumental recital, a song, a poem, or a story. Mother often read excerpts of special Christmas letters to us. Father always read the biblical account and prepared a short devotional. We would then go around the family circle and each one of us would thank God for one thing we were especially grateful for, and we closed with the Lord's Prayer.
>
> After this, we had a short break, for cookies and juice, and then gifts were brought out from various

bedrooms and distributed. We never placed gifts under the tree, so this was a time of great surprises; nobody had even seen the gifts before. The space under the tree was reserved for a beautifully hand-crafted manger scene with a burning candle next to the baby Jesus.[1]

How many of your childhood Christmas presents can you actually remember now? Probably not enough to count on one hand. But we all know that a sudden fragrance can bring back, in living color, an entire day of childhood. Let's give our children those same memory triggers.

FEEDING YOUR FAMILY'S SENSES

Are you a cook? No better time than Christmas to exercise your ability with special Christmas recipes—cookies, fruitcake, fancy pudding—that will forever after remind your kids of those precious childhood Christmases. Resist the temptation to make only the same toll-house or oatmeal cookies you always serve, even if they're family favorites. Instead, search out special Christmas recipes—spicy cookies redolent with cinnamon, ginger, and glazed fruit; fruitcakes (I know, I know—you get at least three fruitcakes a year anyway, and they're usually too rich to eat, and the kids don't like them. But try making one this year. It's a real Christmas experience, and it smells great. Even if you can't eat it.) Special drinks, like eggnog or mulled cider. Pop lots of corn for popcorn balls and popcorn strings for your tree; let your kids eat as much as they want as they string it. Buy a Christmas cookbook for ideas for other baked goods and special seasonal treats. (There are plenty of them. Last night—a few days before Halloween—I browsed through a couple of bookstores. They had several Christmas cookbooks out already: books of Christmas cookies, Christmas beverages, Christmas candies. The library has even more.)

And once you've found your Christmas favorites, then make them only for Christmas, no matter how much your kids beg. Let it be a special treat, a taste and fragrance that will mean "Christmas" to them all their lives.

If your family has an ethnic background, you're doubly blessed. Reinforce your children's (and your own) awareness of your heritage with authentic Christmas dishes from your people's "place." Bob Hudson remembers his mother's braided Swedish coffee cake, with its three strands symbolic of the Trinity. "We discussed that symbolism briefly and matter-of-factly as we ate it," Bob reminisces. "Nothing detailed or threatening, just a simple statement so that my sister and I could understand how all of these traditions led us back to Christ."

Don't know how to cook ethnic foods? So what? Learn! And if your elder relatives can't help you, learn from a book. Don't lose touch with your roots just because you're too busy.

And while you're doing all this cooking (and this is the really hard part), don't exclude your kids. Kids love to cook, and even a difficult dish has at least a few steps a child can handle—stirring in the nuts, kneading the dough, counting out the walnut halves, rolling the dough into balls, brushing the dish with oil, and so on. Kids like nothing better than to be included in what their parents are doing. Sure, it'll take a little longer. But remember that you're in the business of making memories right now. And, with that in mind, I hereby give you permission to jump ahead in this book and read the story that opens chapter 10. Your kids *will* remember this time they spend with you, even if you don't. And it will make a difference to them.

Even if your family doesn't normally prepare a formal Christmas dinner, consider doing it this year—and inviting guests who wouldn't otherwise have much of a Christmas celebration. Strangers? Why not? Chapters 7 and 8 contain more suggestions for reaching out to others.

The holiday kitchen, besides catering to your family's taste buds, also provides some of the holiday's favorite fragrances. But you needn't limit your holiday fragrances to cooking aromas. In these days of scented candles and potpourri, every home can enjoy a variety of holiday fragrances, including evergreen and mulling spices. Of course candles also provide a lovely, atmospheric flame (which you'll need to keep out of the reach of the smallest members of the family).

What about the many sounds that unmistakably tell you what season it is? The jangle of sleigh bells; the tinkle of Salvation Army kettle bells. But probably the most familiar and the most unmistakable is the sound of Christmas carols. Most families already own at least one or two Christmas albums or tapes; consider getting a few more. Check them out of the library if you can't afford to buy them, or trade off for a week at a time with friends. Play them frequently; let them become the background for your Christmas activities.

And not just the recorded versions, either. *Sing.* And if you can't sing, whistle. Few children can resist joining in when a parent sings a beloved song like "Away in a Manger," "Jingle Bells," or "Silent Night." It gives them an outlet for the excitement that's building in them. I've often noticed that overenergetic children (yes, believe it or not, we've occasionally had them in our house) calm down when singing or listening to peaceful songs.

Add other sounds. What about wind chimes or musical Christmas bells that play carols when you pull a string? I've seen Christmas music boxes, and those great strings of large jingle bells attached to your door make every entrance or exit sound festive.

Don't overlook the sense of sight. Decorate your home. Let the kids help with picking out (or, better yet, making) the Christmas decorations. Many books or holiday-issue magazines include directions for making a variety of creative Christmas decorations; check your library. If you lack the time to assemble the raw materials to make the projects described in books, or if you're just not handy enough to handle much do-it-yourselfery, you're in luck: Kits for Christmas decorations abound. A visit to your favorite craft store in the fall should turn up plenty of kits, many simple enough for your children. If you can string beads, you can make Christmas decorations.

Wreaths are a favorite; our family has made wreaths

from evergreen boughs, wild grape vines trimmed with ribbon, and pinecones glued to plywood. The trip into the forest to collect the raw materials is half the fun for us; we've sometimes made a day of it, with picnic lunch, thermos of hot chocolate, and so on. (But listen to the voice of experience: If you plan on heading into the forest to pick up pinecones from the forest floor, do it before the snow falls.) Tack a few sprigs of evergreen or holly up above the doorframes or on the front door. And what child can resist helping to hang Christmas lights, either inside or outside? Buy a few extra strings of lights this year and use them to line windows.

Let the kids paint one of the front windows of your home with a scene of their choice. Use paint made from powdered laundry detergent and water mixed to the consistency of heavy cream, colored with powdered poster paint. They can paint with either brushes or sponges.

Consider doing something different with your tree this year. Ron and Joyce Rogers decorate their tree differently every year—in a way that will have symbolic significance for the family. One year they used only straw ornaments, to remind them of Christ's birth in a stable. They used a straw lamb, straw canes (symbolic of the good Shepherd), and straw stars. Another year, they used only ornaments of copper (representing Christ the man) and gold (for Christ as God and King). Each year they start decorating their tree at the beginning of Advent, each day adding another ornament as a family activity, with the reading of a Scripture verse appropriate for that ornament.

Write out (with your children) Mary's song in Luke 1:46–55 to hang on the wall. Also hang posters and long ribbons and attach all the Christmas cards you've received; hang mistletoe and reinforce your child's sense of belonging with plenty of sloppy kisses—*anything* that reinforces, through your child's senses (and your own, as well) that this is a special time of year.

Most of us agree that television is a wasteland; it's probably the last place we'd expect the find constructive, meaningful visual stimulation for our families. But a number of Christmas specials and movies every year are actually worth watching. Your children will anticipate watching the new ones as well as the old standbys. Why not make it a family activity this year, with popcorn and hot spiced cider? Last year we taped the Christmas specials on our VCR to watch later. That way we weren't at the mercy of network scheduling; we could watch at our convenience, when it fit in with our plans. We could also fast-forward past the commercials, saving time and sparing our children the unnecessary messages of self-indulgence, cheap sexuality, and substance abuse.

Don't forget the seasonal sights and sounds outside your own four walls. All kids love to drive to the local Christmas Tree Lane, for instance, and see all the great decorations. What about driving up into the mountains, if you're lucky enough to have some close by, and enjoying the snowbound scenery? What about live Christmas nativity scenes and singing Christmas trees? And don't forget Christmas pageants, concerts, plays, and parties; in most communities there's no lack of announced activities to attend.

Why is all this so important? Because you want your children to *experience* Christmas in some other way than through their acquisitive natures. These sights, sounds, and smells can provide enjoyable experiences for your family that are far more compatible with a true Christmas celebration than a frenzy of gift receiving.

EXPERIENCING BY DOING

It's December twenty-seventh. You collapse in your chair—and suddenly realize that you haven't spent any real time with your kids in weeks. You've been doing it all for *them,* of course, all the late nights, all the dodging holiday traffic and slogging a mile and a half through muddy, half-frozen slush to the mall from the very last parking spot in the whole blasted parking lot, all for them—but you haven't spent much time with the objects of all that devotion except to get cranky with them sometimes when you just got too tired to be patient anymore.

Here's a simple truth we all know but seldom act on: Kids want our time and our attention more than they want our wealth or our gifts. It's us they want.

The high price our children pay for our overburdened calendars doesn't have to get worse at Christmas. It should get better. Your kids will benefit if you shop less and play more Go Fish. But they'll benefit even more if you find holiday activities that your family can participate in together that will forever after spell C-h-r-i-s-t-m-a-s for you and your kids.

Throughout this book, I've suggested activities such as caroling that can satisfy a number of your holiday objectives, such as exercising compassion and spending time with family and friends. But besides those, you can find a number of seasonal activities. All kids love to drive to your local Christmas Tree Lane, for instance, and see all the great decorations. What about driving up into the mountains, if you're lucky enough to have some close by, and enjoying the snowbound scenery? Or ice-skating or skiing together, or simply building snowmen or having snowball fights? The requirements for successful seasonal activities are simple: they should involve your entire family in close, affectionate activity, and they should be tied to the season.

Another option: as part of your family worship experience, act out parts of the Christmas story. On other nights during Advent, try acting out scenes from Dickens' *A Christmas Carol,* as did Mike Smith and his family. Mike says, "That was a couple of years ago, and the kids still talk about it." This dramatic presentation can be as elaborate (with costumes and sets, which your children will enjoy preparing) or as spontaneous as you choose; either way, the thing to remember is that kids love play-acting—and that preadolescent children have a poor grasp of abstract concepts, but readily understand and remember concrete sights and sounds.

The Swiss psychologist Jean Piaget described these limitations and abilities best. From approximately ages two to five, according to Piaget, children are in the stage he calls *prelogical thought.* Although things are beginning to "make sense" to them, they still operate as if they believe that everything in the world revolves around them; they also have a hard time differentiating between those objects and events they experience and those they imagine. Between the approximate ages of five and twelve, children are in the stage Piaget calls *concrete operations.* Their minds are much like computers at this point, observing, counting, memorizing, organizing, and reorganizing concrete objects and information. But they have a hard time dealing with abstract ideas (obedience, worship, honesty, loyalty, evil, and so on). Most people, somewhere between the ages of eleven and fifteen, enter Piaget's highest category, *formal operations,* at which time they develop the ability to deal with abstractions.

That's why, to reinforce in our children's minds the reason for celebrating Christmas, we should look for family-group experiences and activities that tell the simple Christmas story over and over again.

Yes, all of this takes time—all the more reason to consider alternatives to the frenzy of last-minute gift buying that characterizes the average American Christmas. All the more reason to turn to creative, alternative methods of gift shopping and exchange—to free your Christmas season for family activities.

Hasn't the problem in past years been that you just lacked the time? Or were so busy that any family activities were more like a chore than an enjoyable sharing time? This year, reserve time for such activities. Choose those that are fun, that your children will remember, and that remind you whose birthday it is.

Is the effort it takes to fill your children's Christmas—and your own—with memories, experiences, and activities worth it? If you want them to remember the Christmases of their childhood and to appreciate what Christmas truly means, it is. Ron and Joyce Rogers have gone to much trouble over the years to make their Christmases different from the commercialized pattern set by society. Was it worth it in their family? "Our kids still talk about how we celebrated Christmas when they were children," Joyce explains. "Now, when they come home from college, they still insist that we do the same things we did when they were growing up." Was it worth it? You decide.

Then decide to do the same for your own children, regardless of their ages—and for yourself.

After all, the true meaning of Christmas is not just for kids.

Chapter Seven

Sharing Christmas with Family and Friends

I DON'T LIKE IT, Joyce Rogers thought when she first saw the painting for sale in the shop: Santa Claus kneeling at the manger, worshiping the infant Jesus. *It trivializes Christmas.*

Later she changed her mind. *That's exactly what we're trying to do in our family,* she realized. *We don't want to eliminate the cultural aspects of the American Christmas, but rather to make them subject to Christ. Like all of life, they should find their meaning only in relationship to him.*

Joyce is right. If you've decided to redesign your family Christmas, you'll want to choose the elements of your celebration by that same criterion: Do they, like

Santa in the painting, kneel at the manger? Do they serve Christ?

In the previous chapters of this book, I've discussed ways to choose activities that focus your family's attention on Christ. But the "family" I've been discussing, for the most part, has been the immediate family—those who live under the same roof with us, or those who would if they weren't separated from us due to divorce, schooling, and so on. At Christmas *family* takes on a wider meaning. For many of us in this hectic, overcommitted society, Christmas may be the one time of year—except for the occasional family reunion, wedding, or funeral—when we have much involvement with our extended family.

And that creates a unique opportunity and responsibility: to become evangelistic about Christmas. Celebrating the birth of Christ is, after all, the perfect introduction to the Gospel in our society. It is the one recognition of Christ's worth and work that almost no one objects to. To share it in a meaningful way with as many people as possible is a way of obeying Christ's parting words to his disciples: "You will be my witnesses in Jerusalem, and in all Judea and Samaria, and to the ends of the earth" (Acts 1:8).

Let's explore together ways to share that message of hope and love and joy as Christ suggested: first, to those closest to us—our extended family; next, to those a little further away—friends and acquaintances; and last, in chapter 8, to "the ends of the earth"—those we may never have met before.

ALL IN THE FAMILY

There are good reasons (in addition to evangelism) for sharing our Christmas—and the other aspects of our Christian faith—with our extended family. Not doing so probably weakens our faith. After a recent poll taken in Denmark (in which, incidentally, only 32 percent of those surveyed reported that Christmas had "any religious meaning" for them), sociologist Ole Rijs observed that "the most relevant church rites are those that lead to an ensuing festivity for the extended family and friendship network. Such occasions may be baptisms, confirmations, marriages, burials, or Christmas."[1] Including "the extended family and friendship network" in our observance of religious events—such as Christmas—is one way to reinforce the importance of those events and to strengthen the religious commitment of the participants, ourselves as well as our relatives.

But despite those benefits, throwing open a Christmas celebration to the extended family is easier said than done for many of us. Families are often scattered by hundreds or thousands of miles, and scattered even more irrevocably by angry disputes, or by barriers of professional attainment, educational level, income, or religious belief.

Families not divided by those barriers may be so bound by tradition that any change in the family's Christmas celebration is simply out of the question. Or there may be other, more serious problems in the way your extended family celebrates Christmas: dysfunctional, exploitative behavioral patterns and relationships that create high anxiety for you at Christmastime; high doses of "family guilt" and emotionally charged obligations to do or say certain things or behave in certain ways. Ask yourself: Do you *fear* or *gladly anticipate* your time with your extended family this Christmas? If you fear it, then it's time to consider doing something about it. Even if you make many positive changes in your own personal Christmas, dreaded extended-family obligations can make the holiday season a horror.

Start by identifying those elements of the extended-family Christmas celebration you want to change. Do you feel that you bear an inordinate amount of the burden of responsibility in some way? (For instance: Do your siblings expect you to give up Christmas day to care for aging parents while they celebrate with their in-laws? Does everyone expect you to prepare a first-class Christmas dinner with all the trimmings—single-handedly?) Do you feel oppressed or threatened by some relative you just don't want to see?

Then think up alternatives that will not only eliminate or mitigate the problem you're trying to avoid, but will also contribute a positive alternative. Does no one want to take on the cooking duties? If the fellowship is the important thing, then settle for a pot-luck or a chili dinner—or go out to eat and then spend the day together afterwards. If your siblings are planning to, as always, abandon you and your aged parents on Christmas day, suggest that your family's celebration be on New Year's day instead, when it won't conflict with your siblings' other family responsibilities.

Chapter 11 includes some suggestions on how to

present these plans for change to your extended family. But regardless of how positively and persuasively you present your ideas—asking what they think, showing a willingness to incorporate their ideas into the new plan— the answer may be no. There may be negative behavioral or attitudinal problems too strong to overcome simply by suggesting a good alternative. And even in the healthiest families, tradition may have too strong a hold, particularly on the older members. And in that case, you have a choice to make. You can, if you're able, accept them where they are and continue to participate in your family's traditional Christmas, even though aspects of it may be painful to you. Or you can opt out—decline to participate in any aspects of your extended family's activities that offend or threaten you. Whichever choice you make, you're still free to make any changes you want in the way your immediate family celebrates, and in the way you respond to friends, the community, those in need, and to Christ himself.

Ironically, you might find that your best bet for giving your extended family a more meaningful Christmas is by suggesting more, not less, tradition. That's especially true for those whose families have a definite ethnic background. Exploring the Christmas traditions of that ethnicity can be great fun, can draw the family closer together, and can also give each of you a greater understanding of Christmas. Bob Hudson, well into adulthood, still has vivid childhood memories of his Swedish grandparents taking him to Lutheran Santa Lucia services the week before Christmas—a strongly visual and symbolic experience.

Regardless of your ethnic background—European, South American, Asian, Russian—there are seasonal traditions that would help bind the children in your extended family to their heritage while reinforcing their understanding of Christ's birth. If you don't know much about those traditions yourself, ask your older relatives, research it at the library, or contact the local ethnic organization.

If members of the extended family aren't interested in attending ethnic activities or observing ethnic traditions, propose other ways to share each other's company. Take a chance; suggest that, rather than exchanging presents this year, all of you from near and far invest in a weekend trip to enjoy each other's company, as Cal and Mary Buist do each year with one branch of the family.

Or, if your family is fairly conservative and isn't likely to agree to a major investment of time and money, make sure everyone is included and involved in the old standby—the family Christmas dinner. There'll undoubtedly be some who, because of distance, can't attend. Don't leave them out. Have a tape recorder or video camera on hand, not only to record portions of the festivities but also to record personal messages from the participants to the missing ones.

And that, in fact, is a great idea even apart from the family dinner. If there are relatives or friends you won't be seeing at Christmas, why not prepare for them an audio or video tape, wishing them a merry Christmas from the entire family? Before their daughter's first Christmas, David and Martha Foster had to move away from close friends. But the Fosters recorded the event on videotape and routed it to all of those friends who had missed seeing her open her first presents and experience her first snow.

You and your family can do the same. Younger children especially will love reading a short message for the camera or the microphone or participating in an "interview"—answering questions you ask them about Christmas or about recent activities—or singing Christmas carols. Just remember that the idea is to do more than say hi; you and your family want to communicate to those on the receiving end of this tape or video what Christmas really means. Besides the laughter and the news and the fun, they should hear about the importance of Christ in your Christmas and in your family. Record the reading of the Christmas story by different family members; take turns telling what Christmas stands for.

OUTSIDE THE FAMILY CIRCLE

Mike and Sherry Smith and family were enjoying a pre-Christmas visit with another family when a great idea struck them: Why not act out the Christmas story right here? Kids and parents hustled up costumes and sets and the play was on. As it progressed, Mike noticed that each of the two families had unique gifts that made the play more fun and more successful than either family could have made it alone.

"I realized then," Mike explains, "that we've had the most fun when we've been with another family, and our creativity has been stimulated. There's definitely a synergistic effect."

There is indeed. Most of us have noticed that, at times when our family isn't having much social contact with outside friends, we tend to get in a rut—to think and do the same things. Involving ourselves with outside friends changes that; they stimulate us as we stimulate them, and the results are unexpected and fun.

Spending special social times with close friends is only one way to achieve that synergy. Wayne and Marci Rice and their family found another: a "prayer basket." They write the names of friends and others they know on slips of paper and put them in a basket; at certain times during Advent, each family member takes a slip from the basket and is called upon to share something about the person whose name is on that slip—a memory, a valued and admirable trait about that person, a need, an appreciation. Then the family joins in prayer for those they've discussed.

Cal and Mary Buist have found an additional way to open the family circle. They became aware that many people, including some in their own church, had no family close by with whom to spend Christmas and were spending that day alone. They looked at the richness of their own family's Christmas celebration and realized that they had something to share. They began inviting people into their home for Christmas dinner and activities. "Usually, we choose people who might not have much of a Christmas otherwise—those whose relatives live out-of-state, for instance," Mary explains.

The people you invite don't necessarily have to be

people you know well; in fact, those you *don't* know well often have greater need, for just that reason. That was the case with my family when we first moved to this city several years ago; far from other relatives and new to town, I feared that Christmas might be lonely—especially as my kids began to ask, "Will we see Grandma?" "Will anybody come over?" But I knew no one to invite; everyone seemed busy with family activities in this close-knit community.

I was wracking my brain for ways to make our Christmas more homey when I got a call from a new acquaintance: "We're having a few friends over Christmas Day for dinner and fellowship. Would your family like to join us?"

A small thing? Not to me, not to my kids. The day we had expected to be lonely turned out to be warm and full with new friends. Inviting in friends or even strangers is another way to complete the family circle—with grandma-aged people as well as other little-type people to replace the absent cousins.

In your circle of acquaintances do you know older people who won't have a family surrounding them over the holidays? Adopt them as local "grandparents" to your children. You and your children will benefit (most likely for a longer period than just the Christmas holidays), and you'll bring joy into an older couple's life as well.

Other opportunities arise from the sometimes meaningless habit of exchanging Christmas cards with friends. In recent years more and more families have given it up. Christmas is too busy anyway. Why make it any busier by sending out scores of cards that few consider meaningful?

Good question. And the best answer is that it *can* be made meaningful. Here are some alternatives to the normal practices of sending and receiving cards that may help breathe meaning into your Christmas:[2]

1. Personalize your cards. Photo cards or handmade cards or cards that contain a "Christmas letter" (maybe on stationery illustrated by your children) tend to speak a more personal message to the recipient than those that are merely mass-produced and mass-mailed. Yes, it takes longer and usually requires more foresight. This year, we're designing and writing our own cards and having them hand-set and hand-printed by a friend who has an antique, cold-type press. What's the advantage in that? Besides the fun of it as a family activity—choosing the design, writing and revising the message, and so on—the only advantage is that our message will be from *us,* rather than from a writer at Hallmark.

2. Instead of buying your cards at a local discount store or card shop, buy them from charities such as World Vision, UNICEF, The National Wildlife Federation, and so on. Besides the fact that the money you spend on the cards will be put to good use in funding the activities of those charities, the cards themselves carry a message of concern and compassion to those on your mailing list.

3. Here's a great idea from Alice Lawhead's *The Christmas Book:*

> I have a friend who does not send Christmas cards. She collects the many cards she and her husband receive in a basket. Then, throughout the year, as they have their daily devotions after breakfast, they

draw one card from the basket and pray specifically for the person or family who sent the card. Later in the day she follows up by sending a little preprinted letter explaining what happened, writing a personal note at the bottom. I look forward to receiving my card from Vivian, wondering when my name will be drawn.[3]

Or you might prefer to bring one card a day to the family dinner table and pray for that individual or family as you say grace.

4. Christmas is so busy anyway that many of us who want to send cards, or who want to do something more meaningful with our cards, simply can't find the time. So why send them at Christmas when so much else is going on? If you like the idea of sending annual greetings to your friends and extended family, do it at Thanksgiving or Valentine's Day or Easter. Even if those on your list are a bit puzzled the first year, they'll soon realize what you're up to and will look forward each year to your "Easter Christmas card."

5. Make the most of the cards that have been sent to you; after all, someone has gone to a great deal of trouble and expense to send them. Open them as a family activity, perhaps at the dinner table. Display them in some prominent place; many families mount them on ribbons tacked over doorways or along a mantel. Allow your kids to pick their favorites to decorate their bedroom doors. Stand them on a buffet or endtable or windowsill.

6. If you're burned out on sending cards, skip a year or two. It won't kill you or your friends, even if a few of them have hurt feelings. Then review your list; make

some additions and subtractions and start over. It'll mean more after the breather.

7. Cut your list way down; eliminate all the "social obligation" names from your list, and keep only those with whom you really want to keep in touch. To those, take the time to include a letter. Don't include people you'll see during the season; greet them personally.

Christmas is not a time to be turned inward, away from the world. Despite the emphasis on family activities and family relationships, Christmas is a time for sharing what we have and what we know of Christ with the world, and the world includes our friends.

This book is full of suggestions for activities and gifts that honor Christ. As you plan those activities, include your friends. When you plan a caroling outing or an institutional visit, call your friends and ask if they'd be interested in participating. When you offer your services to a downtown mission, ask how many of your friends you can bring along.

You aren't the only one frustrated that Christmas isn't all it should be. Your friends feel the same way. And you can be a redeeming force in your friends' lives this year by showing them a better way, by inviting them to participate in your joy with you, by making them feel even more a part of your family.

That will be a gift beyond price.

Chapter Eight

Exporting Christmas: Sharing with Strangers

"THIS IS REALLY GOING to screw up our holiday," grumbled nine-year-old Kevin Callahan. Why? Kevin's parents had just announced a change of holiday plans: The Callahan family would spend Thanksgiving and Christmas days serving dinner to the destitute at local shelters. Just what every nine-year-old wants to hear.

It didn't turn out as he had expected. A couple of years later, he shrugged his shoulders and said, "What was so important, after all, about watching college football games on TV at Christmas and Thanksgiving?" Kevin and his brothers, rather than sitting mesmerized by a TV screen, created strategies for these holiday dinners to make them more enjoyable for everyone: People in wheelchairs needed to be carried downstairs to the dining room, tables needed to be set up, plates filled, and later, there was the cleanup.

The response of Kevin and his brothers might surprise those who think of today's young people as single-minded pleasure seekers, but it won't surprise those who are aware of Pulitzer-prize-winning author and psychotherapist Ernest Becker's observation that "Youth was made for heroism and not for pleasure."[1]

Reflecting on Becker's thoughts, sociologist Tony Campolo concluded that, if we lose this generation of young people, it will not be because we didn't entertain them enough. It will be because we didn't *challenge* them enough.

> I'm convinced that young people are turned on by seemingly impossible challenges. I believe that teenagers are thrilled when the evangelist at a youth convention shouts, "If those of us here totally give ourselves to Jesus, we can change the world!" Teenagers hear in such challenges a call of holy crusades in which they can be knights. They hear in the words of the evangelist a call to undertake what they're led to believe is the greatest cause in human history.[2]

For the sake of our children who need noble challenges on which to sharpen themselves, for the sake of us parents who need constant reminders not to be sucked into the pleasant but ungodly values of middle America, for the sake of the Christ whose birthday we celebrate who calls us to deny ourselves, take up our cross, and follow him, our Christmases should not be turned inward, centered on our own desires and comforts, but rather turned outward toward those whose needs range from hunger to homelessness to ignorance of the Gospel.

TO THE ENDS OF THE EARTH

If our Christmas celebration is an act of worship and thanksgiving—in some ways, the archetypal Christian holiday and celebration—and if Christianity is evangelistic in nature (as Acts 1:8 and Matthew 28:16–20 leave little doubt), then the true Christmas spirit of adoration for Christ should be flowing out of our homes and infecting others.

Not all of those "others" need be family members or people we already know. Some can be total strangers, just as the Samaritan served God by ministering to the needs of the stranger he found wounded on the road.

"We are our brothers' keepers," Kenneth Kantzer wrote not long ago.

It is our God-given duty to seek, as best we can, to meet their needs.

Naturally I cannot evaluate with any accuracy all the intricate causes of poverty and human suffering. I certainly don't know the remedies. . . .

Without suggesting for a moment every Christian must do the same, I know certain things are right, and I can do them. I can set my lifestyle a mite below the average in my community. The money I do spend, I can use for truly worthwhile things and not for items that gratify pleasure at the expense of my moral and spiritual growth. I can contribute a minimum of one-tenth of my income to causes directly related to God's kingdom and not to general charity. To the extent of my ability, I can help out those I see to be in need even if it requires that I make some significant sacrifices. I can vote for just governments, honest administrators, and laws that prevent the exploitation of the innocent, the handicapped, and the powerless. And I can seek to find helpful ways of serving others.[3]

Here are some suggestions for being a Samaritan—your brother or sister's keeper—this Christmas:

SERVING THE POOR IN YOUR COMMUNITY

I am writing this in the air, flying home from a conference at the convention center in downtown Washington, D.C. Fresh in my mind as I write are the homeless, the "bums," the panhandlers who stopped me at every street corner to ask for money for a "cup of coffee" or a bed for the night. Walking to my hotel each evening, I passed the men curled up on cardboard boxes in doorways. On my way to fine restaurants for lunch or dinner, I passed men and women scavenging in trash cans, picking through the remains of the box lunches some of the conferees had carelessly discarded.

And when they asked for money, I said no, running

over in my mind the standard excuses evangelicals and middle-class people in general use in those situations: *If I give my money to everybody who asks me for it on this trip, I won't have enough to get home on. Besides, how do I know they won't just spend it on drugs or booze? And it won't really help the overall problem anyway: "Give a man a fish, and you feed him for a day. Teach him to fish, and you feed him for the rest of his life."*

Reasonable excuses, actually. Good points. But sometimes God asks us to do unreasonable things. And perhaps giving is something that benefits the object of our generosity less than it benefits us. We may indeed have fed him only for a day, but we've helped establish in ourselves a pattern of selfless thought that, once established, will stay with us forever.

And so I offer this Christmas experiment: This year, during the Advent season, give to everyone who asks of you. Not much, perhaps, but something. Do it reflexively, without thinking, without asking the usual reasonable questions. Many of those who ask will be, of course, our Christian brothers and sisters whom Christ commanded us to love. For them, how could we do less? The others—the one who comes to your door seeking donations, the panhandler, the Salvation Army bell ringer—are certainly no more humble or homeless than a poor babe in a manger.

Few, I suspect, of those who read this book will try that experiment. I've suggested it to several friends over the past couple of years, and heard predictable, reasonable responses:

"*All* who ask of me? Impossible! Do you realize how

many direct-mail solicitations I get this time of year? I must be on every mailing list in the country!"

"But what about the Hare Krishnas and the Mormons? How can I contribute to them?"

"But that violates my principle of never responding positively to phone solicitations."

Reasonable responses, every one. I'll let my suggestion stand, nevertheless. And for those who don't want to try it, I suggest instead that, for your own sake, and for Christ's whose birthday we're celebrating, let your generosity toward others, measured in whatever currency you like, take a giant step forward during this season.

Your family might follow the example of Kevin Callahan's family and pitch in during the holiday season at shelters for the homeless, assisting those ministries that serve the castoffs of society. If you make this choice, your children, like Kevin and his brothers, may be somewhat resistant at first. Nancy Roberts makes several suggestions to help create a caring, compassionate atmosphere in your family, based on the experiences of families like the Callahans:[4]

1. *Make social concern and compassion a matter of lifestyle.* Model the concerns you want your children to share. Roberts cites studies that indicate that individuals who participate in social causes are likely to have grown up in families that participated in social causes.

2. *Provide opportunities to see the other half of society.*

Mark, 15, couldn't understand why his father spent one night a month at a local shelter for the homeless. Why couldn't these people just go out and get a job, he wanted to know. His father told him, "Before you pass judgment, come with me to the shelter for a night." The experience demolished many of the boy's stereotypes of the poor. Now he no longer questions his father's involvement.[5]

3. *Practice justice at home.* Your kids aren't likely to be impressed with your attempts to work for social justice outside the home if you're an arbitrary, hostile tyrant at home or if you're always gone—off somewhere "doing good." Be honest with yourself: If you feel God calling you to a ministry of justice and compassion, is that calling any less important inside your own family?

4. *Don't force opinions.* Give your kids opportunity to speak their minds—even if you hear, "Why are we giving away all of our time and money to some undeserving poor person when I really want a CD player for Christmas?" They're more likely to "own" their convictions if they arrive at them on their own.

You might look for opportunities for children to help other children. Your church probably provides food or clothing or other needed items to underprivileged families at Christmas; participate in that effort not only by donating money and goods, but also by helping to locate those families and by delivering the food and clothing— as a family. Your children will benefit greatly—and they will remember those visits far longer than they will remember what they themselves receive as gifts this year. Susan Schaeffer Macaulay still remembers those experiences from her childhood in Switzerland:

We always cooked a Christmas dinner for some villager. Mother would ask around and find someone who was very needy. We would have one roast dinner a year, ourselves, but, even so, my mother would take a roast of meat, and we'd put it in a box with lots of extra goodies, like a nice plant and other food. To deliver it we'd hike through the snow— together as a family. One year it must have been about a two-hour hike, way up into the mountains, on Christmas Eve day. We went to visit a little boy lying on a wooden bed who had been in the same room for nearly two years; he had a tubercular hip. The family had nothing. No running water, just potatoes and a bit of milk from their one cow. I shall always remember this little boy's eyes as we unpacked our things.

Sometimes we went to old people, and sometimes they'd say, "But why are you doing this?" We children would do the talking, "We remember the birth of Christ in this way. He came to bring us his gift and we wanted to bring you a gift at Christmas."[6]

Sheila Schuller Coleman, daughter of well-known pastor, media personality, and author Robert Schuller, suggests leading your children in a giving exercise early in the Christmas season:

Two Christmases ago I was depressed on Christmas morning because my children had received so many presents—and they'd only been to one side of the family, my husband's side. We hadn't even gone to my parents' yet to open their presents. It really, really bothered me—that my kids had so much. So last year, about the first week in December, the boys and I went through their drawers. We pulled out clothes that no longer fit them. We went through all their toys and pulled out those they had outgrown. Then they went with me to a thrift store and we donated their things so that other children could have them. The boys actually carried the bags into the store. I wanted them to gain a sense of giving something on Christmas—as well as receiving. They really understood and were bothered by the fact that some kids didn't get things for Christmas. I think it was important for them to give before they received.[7]

This suggestion from *The Alternate Celebrations Catalogue* might work in your family, too, and it's a good way to involve other families with children:

Last Christmas, we got together and gave a party for all of our children. The party was devised around the plan to have the children wrap their own toys to give to other children. We read to them from the Bible about what Jesus said about love and giving. . . . The children had brought a tremendous amount of gifts that they wanted to give away: toys, books, clothing. When all the things were wrapped, we took the children and the gifts to the home of a family, fatherless, with 16 children. They understood that they were not taking these gifts to show that they were good boys and girls, but rather because Christ could show love through them. They were humble, and I don't think that they will ever forget the experience.[8]

It is, indeed, unlikely that your children will forget the experience of exercising compassion toward others at Christmas.

Thousands of churches across the country participate in Prison Fellowship Angel Tree®, a program in which church members—often as a family project—buy Christmas gifts for local children of prisoners. Prison Fellowship staff work with prisoners, collecting names and addresses of their children. It's a personalized program; church volunteers call the homes and ask for specific gift needs or wishes—usually one item of clothing and one toy—of specific children.

The program builds bridges in several ways: between prisoner and child, because the gifts are presented to the children as being from their absent parent; between churches and unchurched people, because volunteers deliver the gifts—and Gospel comic books—personally, either arranging to deliver them to the homes or sponsoring a Christmas party for the prisoners' children. As church families follow up these initial visits, prisoners' families see the love of Christ in action.

Prison Fellowship's address is listed, along with other social action agencies, at the end of this chapter. Families may participate even if their churches don't.

INTERNATIONAL OPPORTUNITIES: AS CLOSE AS THE MAILBOX

Sometimes those who are "less fortunate" than we are our co-workers in Christ. Marlene LeFever suggests adopting a missionary family with children about the same ages as your own.[9] As a family project, support that family in a variety of ways: praying for them regularly and writing to encourage them, for instance, with each child writing to the children of corresponding age. Each month, throughout the year, put a little money aside (as a family, with each child encouraged to add some of his or her own) to buy that family something special for Christmas.

One of the best gifts that your family members can give to each other—and to Christ—is the support of an underprivileged child. Compassion International, World Vision, and many other organizations (again, addresses at the end of the chapter) enable your family to provide the monthly support—food, educational materials, medical supplies, clothes—for one child in poverty; all for around twenty dollars a month. It's a continuing commitment; the giving lasts all year long. And so does the reminder, for the whole family, that the baby in the manger was not Santa Claus, the god-of-what-I-can-get, but rather someone who taught us, by his example, to give of ourselves for the benefit of others.

If your family decides to support such a child, here's another idea: Ask the missions agency you choose whether it would be possible to send a small Christmas "care package" to the child you'll be supporting. If so, send it early and include simple, durable toys, clothes, books in the appropriate language (if you can get them) including a Bible, and other items the agency suggests. Your own children will enjoy helping to put together this package for a child they've never seen. Some agencies find packaged gifts impractical but encourage extra cash gifts at Christmas, which local missions workers use to meet the child's specific needs.

Then obtain a photo of the child from the sponsoring agency and place it in a prominent place during the Christmas holiday—a reminder of the "adopted" member of the family. We place ours right next to the crèche itself, so that it's clearly visible during our Christmas Eve birthday celebration.

INSTITUTIONAL VISITS

Visiting those confined to institutions during the holidays used to be a matter of charity and compassion for me. Now it has a more personal meaning.

Last year I was diagnosed with leukemia. Because leukemia weakens the immune system, much like AIDS, I contracted a severe blood infection that spread into my spinal column, causing spinal meningitis. For the first time in my life, I was hospitalized for treatment—for several weeks.

At first I was too ill to care where I was. But as my fever and nausea subsided and I began to be conscious for longer periods of time, as the doctors brought in one horrifying test result after another, as I watched one bag after another of someone else's blood flowing into my veins, my despair grew. I began contemplating an early death, wondering what would happen to my wife, my children.

The despair was eventually replaced by something I'd never experienced before: boredom. I'm an active person;

there's never enough time in the day for all the things I enjoy. Suddenly I was unable to do any of them. My hospital room became a prison. When I was strong enough, I paced in my room or dragged my I.V. stand down the hospital corridor, a surgical mask over my face. I stood in front of the window, looking out, remembering the feel of the wind in my face, humming (I'm serious!):

> *And at night, through the bars,*
> *I gaze at the stars,*
> *And I long for your kisses in vain*
> *A piece of stone I will use for my pillow*
> *As I sleep in these shackles and chains.*

Believe me, it wasn't funny at the time. And the memory of that despair and boredom came flooding back a week ago when I received a letter from the Children's Leukemia Foundation of Michigan asking if I'd be willing to volunteer to visit leukemia patients in our local hospitals a couple of times a month for their support and encouragement. My life is plenty busy already; I was on the verge of declining guiltily when I heard that faint echo: "I was sick . . . and you did not look after me. . . . Whatever you did not do for one of the least of these, you did not do for me" (Matt. 25:43, 45).

Others are in that same bed now, feeling that same despair, that same boredom. If I can help them, I will. It will be a part of my Christmas this year. And perhaps my kids would care to go along.

Those who are institutionalized during the holidays— those who are in hospitals, orphanages, mental institutions, prisons, or nursing homes, for instance—face a disappointing holiday season regardless of how diligently the staff attempts to provide some Christmas cheer. You can help immensely by your visit. A few small presents for children in cancer or orthopedic wards or children's hospitals, delivered by your own (or your children's) hands, can bring a smile to a child in pain. A few carols sung to elderly, bedridden patients in nursing homes can take them away from their present circumstances and remind them of happier days.

And your children, participating with you in these visits, will gain an awareness of the needs of others that they might not gain any other way. When I took my Young Life group caroling at homes for the elderly, the kids often said afterward that they'd had no idea that many older people lived in such drab, monotonous, anonymous surroundings, many of them in pain or wandering the halls in the half-light of confused memory, not even remembering their own names. Yes, it can be a sobering experience to be exposed to the needs of others, but let's give our children the opportunity to lighten someone else's burden.

OTHER ENCOURAGEMENT TO STRANGERS

Caroling. Does your church provide "family" caroling opportunities? Some open the activities to the youth group only. Don't let that deter you; organize your own caroling evening, involving other families. Visit shut-ins as well as institutions, those who need encouragement as well as new church members. Offer hot chocolate, popcorn, and socializing when the caroling is over.

Christmas cards. You probably send cards to a long list of people—most of whom are family or friends or co-workers. This year, consider adding a few names to that list, names of people you might not even know: prisoners, missionaries, people in pain or sorrow. It isn't hard to get their names from friends or your church or local ministries. Send a card with a short message of encouragement and a promise to pray for them—then follow through. Here's an opportunity to make your card sending count for something extra.

Birthday Party for Jesus. If your neighborhood has plenty of kids, you can assume that many of them will not hear a clear presentation of Christ's birth this Christmas—unless you provide it. Consider throwing a birthday party for Jesus and inviting the neighborhood kids. Let some of them help you plan it, suggesting activities and songs they think Jesus would like at his party. Explain to them, briefly and simply (!) the concepts for giving gifts to Christ that we discussed in chapters 2 and 3, and encourage them to plan a gift for him for the party. Read the Christmas story aloud; act it out (involving all the children) using simple, impromptu costumes; sing Christmas carols (as well as "Happy Birthday"); include all the elements of any normal birthday party, with some Christmas touches thrown in—games, treats, a cake, prizes.[10] And each child who attends will, maybe for the first time, hear what Christmas is really about.

Entertaining. Surely your church knows of some local needy families or residents of group homes or foster homes or rest homes who won't be eating much of a Christmas dinner this year. If not, contact a local ministry to the underprivileged. Most parents feel a little uneasy about opening the family circle that large. Most kids are excited by it. Even shy children, though they may not say much, are happy to have guests in their home, even guests they've never met.

GIVE THE BEST

Most of us practice giving at some level. Often, however, we're like the people who donated goods to be sent to my friend Becky's family when she was a child and her parents were missionaries in the Philippines. "We were glad to get whatever they could send," she said, "but unfortunately much of it was unusable—rags, really. Things so badly broken we couldn't fix them. And I'll never forget the time we got a big plastic bag full of teabags—used teabags. Taped to the bag was a little note: 'These should be good for a second cup.'"

"We give the wrong things," notes Alice Lawhead.

> We give what is left over, we give what doesn't fit, we give what is worn out, we give what is broken. . . .
>
> Is it any wonder we are unsatisfied with our benevolence? Are we willing to see the face of Christ on each shopper at the Goodwill store, on each poor child who will receive a doll through the "Christmas for Kids" program, on each "bum" who walks through the food line at the Salvation Army on Christmas Day?

If so, we will give for different reasons, and we will give different things. . . . We will give away the best; we will give away the first. . . .[11]

If we're going to be evangelistic about Christmas this year, if our excitement about the message of the manger is going to erupt out of us in laughter and singing and joy to "Jerusalem, and . . . all Judea and Samaria, and to the ends of the earth" (Acts 1:8), let's not be cheap about it. Let's share with strangers with the same generosity we would extend if they were our children, if they were our parents, if they were our brothers and our sisters.

Because they are.

AGENCIES FOR SOCIAL ACTION[12]

Compassion International
P.O. Box 7000
Colorado Springs, CO 80933
(719) 594-9900

Evangelical Association for the Promotion of Education
P.O. Box 238
Saint Davids, PA 19087
(215) 341-1722

Food for the Hungry, Inc.
P.O. Box E
Scottsdale, AZ 85252
(800) 2-HUNGER

Holt International Children's Services
P.O. Box 2880
Eugene, OR 97402
(503) 687-2202

Prison Fellowship Angel Tree®
P.O. Box 17500
Washington, DC 20041
(800) 762-2551

World Vision
919 West Huntington Drive
Monrovia, CA 91016
(818) 357-7979

Chapter Nine

How to Pick a Gift for Your Spouse

WE'VE SEEN IT IN SITCOMS a dozen times: Christmas morning. The wife demurely unwraps her present from her grinning husband; she opens the box and lifts out—a sweater? Tickets to a play? No—a fishing reel.

"Thanks, dear," she says quietly. "Just what I wanted."

"It'll be great!" he says. "Now we can go fishing together when I get my new boat! And if you don't like that reel, I'll trade you. I've been wanting one like that for a long time." Then he grabs from under the tree his present from his wife; he rips the paper off in a single motion, sends the box lid sailing across the room, and

finds—shotgun shells? Hunting boots? Golf clubs? No—
a sport coat and tie. He holds them up. "Great," he says
morosely.

"I knew you'd like them," she beams. "Don't you
love that color? It's your color."

He's not interested in the color, any more than she's
interested in fishing. If they're kind and understanding
spouses, they'll realize that these gifts are important to
the one who chose them, and they'll wear or use them to
please someone they love. If they're not, they'll get
grumpy and throw the fishing reel and sport coat into a
dark corner of the closet, never to be seen again. Waste of
money.

And a waste also of a great opportunity for that
husband and wife to nourish and encourage each other,
but that opportunity was wasted back when the gifts were
chosen.

CHERISHING AND NOURISHING

Dr. Gary Oliver, in his article "Growing Healthy
Marriages," examines Ephesians 5:29 (NKJV), an important passage concerning marital relationships: "No one
ever hated his own flesh, but nourishes and cherishes it,
just as the Lord does the church."

What does it mean to "nourish" a spouse? *Nourish* is
a behavioral term, as Dr. Oliver points out; it describes
not simply how we feel, but how we are to act. To
illustrate, he tells of visiting a nursery to buy several
houseplants. The clerk gave him detailed instructions

about how much light, water, and fertilizer each plant required, but in his enthusiasm he didn't listen.

On my way out the nursery door, I picked up a packet of fertilizer spikes and took my plants home. The instructions said to use one spike for an eight-inch pot. Because I wanted the plants to grow quickly, I decided to give them as much nourishment as possible. I put three spikes in each plant instead of one.

Knowing that plants need water, I gave my plants more water than any plant deserved. "Like a River Glorious," I watered those plants. I was sure that in no time they would grow, and I would see new buds and leaves.

In several weeks all of my plants were dead. . . . I was convinced I had faithfully nourished each one. But obviously I hadn't nourished them at all. I had killed them.[1]

His point, as it applies to marriage, should be clear: To nourish our spouses, as God's Word instructs us, requires more than giving them what we think they need. Too often, what we think they need is a reflection of what we want—just as Gary Oliver wanted his plants to grow quickly for his own satisfaction—and we end up at Christmas giving our spouses fishing reels when they want microwaves or sexy lingerie when they want new stereo cabinets for the family room or the complete symphonies of Beethoven when they want new skis. And when that happens,

. . . our spouses aren't overwhelmed with gratitude and awe by our thoughtfulness. As a result, we become frustrated, disappointed and discouraged. Our desire was to nourish, but their response is as lifeless as my dead plants.

Nourish does not mean giving others what you think they need or want. Quality nourishment involves stopping, looking, listening, and studying the person you love. Taking the time to do this helps you know what your wife or husband really needs and wants.

Nourish involves learning the love language of your beloved and . . . [loving] in ways meaningful to him or her. Often what says "love" to you, what excites you, what brings you great joy differs greatly from what says "love" to your partner.[2]

Good advice as you choose your gifts for your spouse this Christmas. Resist the temptation to satisfy your own needs and desires in the gift you choose. That setting aside of yourself is a gift in itself, symbolized by the physical gift you choose.

Often, in choosing our gifts for our children, we envision their faces as they open the gifts; we anticipate with pleasure their happiness. As you choose a gift for your spouse this year, anticipate the look on his or her face as that gift is opened, that symbol of the setting aside of yourself, that gift that truly nourishes, based on the personality and tastes of the recipient rather than of the giver.

That gift might be a sweater, a book, or a food processor. Those material things meet needs and can speak love. But the real struggles in most marriages go deeper than kitchen appliances, and in this chapter I'd like to suggest some gifts that are much harder to give than a trash compactor, but that will truly nourish your spouse and your marriage.

Christmas is an opportunity to say to your spouse, "Our marriage is the most important earthly relationship in my life. I'm willing to invest in it, because I want it not only to survive, but to get even better than it is. This gift is a symbol of my love." Don't pass up that opportunity this Christmas.

Don't settle for the gift of a new bathrobe and slippers. Give the gift of a better marriage.

Easier said than done, you may be thinking. *My marriage is in such tough shape it'll take more than a clever gift to fix it. And I don't know whether my spouse is even interested in my choice of gifts.* You're not alone. The institution of marriage is in bad shape; the divorce rate is sky-high, and we all know of marriages that are teetering on the brink. I know first-hand how fragile marriages are in these times; my first marriage ended in divorce, and I approached the writing of this chapter with trepidation. Do I, who have blown one marriage already, have any right to suggest to anyone how to pick a gift for their spouse?

I make no claims to expertise in matters marital; I often wonder in these troubled times whether there *is* such thing as an expert in marriage. I offer in this chapter not advice but suggestions, some of them from those "expert" sources that have been of most help to me, and some from my own experience—of what doesn't work as well as of what does. If I sometimes sound stern, it isn't self-righteousness; it's my anger at my own failures. And my prayer for your marriage as you read is the same as my prayer for mine as I write—that God will use these simple ideas to strengthen the marriages of any of us who try them.

THE GIFT OF TIME

Many marriages fail because of the kids—not because the partners were too little concerned about their kids' welfare, but because they were *too* concerned. They spent nearly all their time, in fact, working for the kids' benefit—to the detriment of their own relationship.

The problem, you see, is that we adults—especially Christian adults, those of us who can quote "If anyone would come after me, he must deny himself and take up his cross daily and follow me" (Luke 9:23)—are *too good* at denying ourselves. We put in long hours earning a living for our families. Then in the evenings it's grocery shopping or mowing the grass or fixing the car and then helping the kids with their homework, maybe some clothes washing, and we fall into bed exhausted. Maybe there'll be some perfunctory lovemaking—with all the appetite and passion we'd have for a hamburger at Mickey D's—before we fall asleep without another word or maybe with a mumbled comment about taking the car in for a tune-up.

We make a virtue of this. We tell ourselves we're just sacrificing for the good of our families—meaning, of course, our children. But what we're doing is denying our children the model of a vibrant, healthy marriage on which to base their own. Do we really want our children to live lives as lackluster as ours? We're also denying our spouses, whom we claim to love, the joy of our loving support and attention.

Our families are suffering for our misplaced self-sacrifice. It's time we started putting our marriages second on our priority lists, right after God.

"But I place a high priority on my marriage!" you protest.

Do you? How much time in the past week have you devoted to your marriage, and your marriage alone—uninterrupted, undistracted, loving and communicating time with your spouse? There wasn't much, was there? If you're like me, there was probably less than you were willing to admit. Well—there's the measure of the priority we place on our marriages. Everything we gave more time to—including soap operas and lawn mowing—we consider more important.

For the sake of your family, reverse that trend. And you can reverse it at Christmas through your choice of a gift for your spouse. Some suggestions:

1. Give your spouse a calendar. But not just any calendar. Buy an attractive wall calendar or weekly appointment calendar, and then customize it by marking times throughout the year (or if you have a hard time planning that far ahead, through the first three months) specifically set aside for the two of you to spend together alone. Sure, mark some family time to spend with the kids, too, but remember those families where marriages have fallen apart because the parents never got a chance to be together apart from the kids.

You might want to pencil in three times a week when you can simply talk for at least a few minutes about how things are going; this seems to be easier to remember if you make it a regular time each week: Tuesday for ten minutes at seven in the morning, just before you wake the kids up, and so on. You might want to designate at least an hour a week for a short "date" away from the house that will allow you to discuss some tougher issues than you have time for in your ten-minute sessions during the week.

But don't make empty promises to this person you love. When you've marked those times and given them to your spouse, *allow no interference!* Once you start letting other concerns bump your one-on-one time with your spouse, it will get bumped every time, because there's always something out there "more important": a ball game for one of your kids, a church meeting, a meeting with a client.

Even time with the kids, as important as it is, shouldn't displace marital togetherness and communication. Your kids will grow up and move out. The nest will be empty—except for that man or woman with whom you've shared a bed. What kind of relationship will you have with that person when you're the only two left in the house? "Well, stranger, we haven't spent much time together the past twenty-five years since we got married, but there's just the two of us left, so what do you say we talk a little bit and get to know each other?" If you haven't done better than that, you'll probably be talking to yourself.

2. Give your spouse a date. Gary Oliver, in the article mentioned at the beginning of this chapter, suggests planning at least two dates a month—real dates, dates that take up a whole evening. One of them could be planned by the husband, and one by the wife. Give those date nights to your spouse as a Christmas present, either by marking them on your Christmas-gift calendar or by giving them in a coupon.

3. Give your spouse a weekend. Sometimes you need more than a few minutes here, an hour there, and the occasional date. You need another honeymoon. You need to do nothing for a couple of leisurely days but enjoy each other, letting somebody else do the cooking and the cleaning and watch the kids. You need a weekend away.

My guess is that most couples probably need a weekend away, all by themselves, at least three times a year. Why not make one of those weekends a Christmas present? Not right at Christmas, probably, since you'll just be too busy. Instead, give your spouse a card that encloses a coupon: "Good for one free surprise on March 3." When your spouse presents you with the coupon on March 3, a Friday, you tell her to pack her bags; you're off for the weekend and won't be back till Sunday afternoon. You've made all the arrangements ahead of time, of course, including baby-sitting.

But remember to *nourish* your spouse with this weekend, and that means, for one thing, that you've planned the weekend around things you both can enjoy together, not around your tastes alone. It also means that you might not want to surprise your spouse with this idea. How spontaneous is your spouse? Some people thrive on the unexpected, while others plan their lives carefully and resent disruptions. If your spouse is likely to resent a surprise, you might explain in a Christmas card that you want to spend a weekend together in February or March and would like some help in planning it.

Surprise or not, a weekend away is a great gift. Be sure to give it the best chance of success by being sensitive to your spouse's personality.

THE GIFT OF TEAMWORK

Why not give your spouse a team jersey this Christmas?

Uh, great idea, Dave, you might be saying, *but my wife really isn't into sports. That would excite her about as much as that fishing reel you were talking about.*

But it might be different if you got one for each of you, with the same colors and team markings. Whenever you wear them, you'll be reminded that you're on the same team.

Marital conflicts too often are viewed as a win-lose proposition. I've got to outshout you, to bully you into giving in so that we can do things the way *I* think they need to be done. That's even more pronounced in stepfamilies, where it's usually not just a personal difference of opinion, but two family systems in conflict.

Let's look at a different model: You and your spouse

are on the same team. It isn't possible for one of you to lose and the other to win. If one of you loses, you both lose. If one goes off after a disagreement feeling unheard, unappreciated, unloved, alone, then the other certainly hasn't won, because the whole family has lost.

You're working toward the same goal. Keep that goal in mind, and remember that reaching it involves cooperation, mutual support (much as on a basketball team, when team members touch one another after a good play or reassure a team member who's made a mistake), and compromise. When the two of you hammer out a compromise decision that allows you both to feel good, you've both won.

Otherwise, you both lose.

What a Christmas gift to your spouse—to put that realization into practice in your family this year! If you succeed, maybe next Christmas you both deserve a trophy: "Parenting Team of (year)."

THE GIFT OF HELP IN CREATING A STRONGER MARRIAGE

How encouraging it is for one spouse to see the other investing in the marriage. Tickets to a seminar on marital conflict solving, reservations for a marriage enrichment weekend, books on communication between spouses—all of these communicate commitment and love.

And there's something a little more frightening that also communicates commitment and love. In a modern

Christian marriage facing stressful times, it's typical to find one partner who thinks, *We need some counseling if this marriage is to survive,* and one partner who thinks, *Not on your life. We don't need counseling; we can't afford counseling; we're not going to get counseling.*

In the past twenty years, we've all seen an increasing number of those marriages—our own, for some of us—dissolve. And we've heard one or both of the ex-partners say, "There just wasn't anything I could do about it. The problems were too big. It was beyond me."

But there was something they could have done about it. They could have sought out counseling. And that may be the most important gift you can give your spouse this year.

Whoa. I'm treading on thin ice here. Many Christians, especially men (who tend to find it difficult to talk about feelings and deeply personal issues anyway), resist the idea of marriage counseling. Even in the midst of intense emotional pain resulting from marital friction, many spouses say, "I don't want somebody else messing with our problems." "I can't talk about this with a stranger." "It's so expensive; we can't afford it." If your marriage is struggling (and that may mean, if your spouse thinks your marriage is shaky, even if you don't see it that way), you can't afford to do without it.

A counselor can help you identify the problems, decide just how big they really are (remember, Goliath looked pretty big to David, too), and give you an unbiased, informed perspective on how to deal with them.

Of course, this gift works only if you're the one

who's been resisting the idea. If it's your *spouse* who's been resisting counseling, he or she won't exactly relish this gift; it will be seen as an attempt to manipulate. In that case, settle for a less-threatening alternative—a marriage enrichment weekend or seminar.

Either way, the opportunity to improve your marriage is well worth the investment of time and money. This Christmas can be the turning point you look back to years from now.

THE GIFT OF COMMUNICATION

Communication gets a lot of lip service (no pun intended) in most marriages but little investment. "If we just talked about this more, we'd be much better off," we say, but we don't make the time to talk.

"You never listen to me! All we ever do is argue!" we complain, but we don't try to find out why; we don't invest the time and effort it takes to identify the negative communication patterns and their causes and introduce new, more positive patterns.

"Why don't you ever tell me how you're feeling? You never open up to me," we lament—but perhaps our spouses have reasons not to open up. Maybe our own negative communication habits (such as jumping all over them when they really speak their minds) have taught them to keep quiet.

In short, communication suffers not only because we don't set aside time for it, but also because we lack the skills that encourage open and honest communication.

This Christmas, give your spouse the gift of improved communication. How do you do that? For starters, indicate your interest and commitment. Buy a couple of books on marital communications as gifts from you to both you and your spouse.[3] You might write out a certificate, pledging to be available to your spouse anytime he or she needs to talk. (And before you say, "No, that's impractical. Sometimes I'm too busy and can't just drop what I'm doing," ask yourself what your priorities are. Is whatever you're afraid to drop or leave, even your job, worth more than your marriage?)

And when you've made the commitment, stick with it. Don't signal bad faith to your spouse by making promises you don't keep. If you've said you're going to listen more and jabber less, listen more and jabber less. Be strict with yourself. Don't hide behind the excuse that your spouse's bad communication habits are what's fouling up your marriage; make sure that *your* communication habits are an example. Follow these ten guidelines from H. Norman Wright's book *Communication: Key to Your Marriage,* and your spouse will likely follow suit.

MARRIAGE COMMUNICATION GUIDELINES
Proverbs 18:21; 25:11; Job 19:2; James 3:8–10;
1 Peter 3:10

1. Be a ready listener and do not answer until the other person has finished talking. Proverbs 18:13; James 1:19

140

2. Be slow to speak. Think first. Don't be hasty in your words. Speak in such a way that the other person can understand and accept what you say. Proverbs 15:23, 28; 21:23; 29:20; James 1:19

3. Speak the truth always but do it in love. Do not exaggerate. Ephesians 4:15–25; Colossians 3:9

4. Do not use silence to frustrate the other person. Explain why you are hesitant to talk at this time.

5. Do not become involved in quarrels. It is possible to disagree without quarreling. Proverbs 17:14; 20:3; Romans 13:13; Ephesians 4:31

6. Do not respond in anger. Use a soft and kind response. Proverbs 14:29; 15:1; 25:15; 29:11; Ephesians 4:26, 31

7. When you are in the wrong, admit it and ask for forgiveness. James 5:6. When someone confesses to you, tell them you forgive them. Be sure it is forgotten and not brought up to the person. Proverbs 17:9; Ephesians 4:32; Colossians 3:13; 1 Peter 4:8

8. Avoid nagging. Proverbs 10:19; 17:9; 20:5

9. Do not blame or criticize the other person. Instead, restore ... encourage ... edify. Romans 14:13; Galatians 6:1; 1 Thessalonians 5:11. If someone verbally attacks, criticizes or blames you, do not respond in the same manner. Romans 12:17, 21; 1 Peter 2:23; 3:9

10. Try to understand the other person's opinion. Make allowances for differences. Be concerned

about their interests. Philippians 2:1–4; Ephesians 4:32[4]

Make better communication in your marriage both a Christmas gift and a New Year's resolution for the coming year and every year thereafter.

Chapter Ten

Long-Distance Christmases: Something Is Better Than Nothing

James Boswell, the famous biographer of Samuel Johnson, had a favorite childhood memory of a day spent fishing with his father, who rarely spent time with young James. For James, that day was a glowing memory of father and son together doing something they both enjoyed. It held great importance for him, and he referred to it often in his writing.

Later, a researcher decided to check the father's diary to see if he mentioned the day. The entry was short: "Took James fishing. A day wasted."[1]

I have sometimes used that story to illustrate the careless indifference many parents have to the little things that make so much difference to their children. I am using it for a different purpose in this chapter—to encourage parents who don't have much time to spend with their children: long-distance parents.

Undoubtedly Mr. Boswell should have spent more time with his son, and undoubtedly he should have been more sensitive to James's desires and needs. But look at the far-reaching effect of the little time he did spend; look how important and precious that time was to James the child—and James the man.

It reminds me of the encouraging message Mike Yaconelli, youth worker and trainer of youth workers, gives to volunteers, those harried individuals who hold down a full-time job, try to give their families what they need, and yet still find a few hours a week to be there for someone else's children—but can't help feeling guilty that they aren't doing more, aren't spending more time changing lives. And Mike's message is this: "Something is better than nothing."

Something is better than nothing. A glad thought to overworked youth workers and a glad thought also to parents who do not have custody of some or all of their children who may live many miles away, parents who struggle to find time to do more than give their children a five-minute phone call of encouragement during the week. Those parents can at least take comfort in this: That five-minute phone call is something. And something is better than nothing.

A simple idea. But if you're a long-distance parent,

how often have you not written to your kids for a month because you couldn't find time to write a "real letter"? A postcard would have been something, and something is better than nothing. How often have you canceled a visit because your schedule was so hectic you'd have only an hour or two to spend together? That's enough time to take them out for a hamburger, and that's something, and something is better than nothing. How often have you not called on the day you'd planned to because you got too busy and only had a few minutes to talk? A few minutes is enough to say, "Hello. I love you," and that's something, and something is better than nothing.

We long-distance parents tend to live under a constant cloud of guilt that we're not doing more for our kids. As a result of that guilt, we do even less because we consider our efforts so paltry they're not even worth the energy. I've known long-distance parents who see their children only once every few years, who call once or twice a year. Why—because they don't love their children? No. Because they've given up. Because they don't think the few minutes here, the weekend there, will make any difference at all. Because it's too frustrating trying to be a part of a child's life from a distance, and because often it doesn't seem that the kids care one way or the other, anyway.

But that one day's fishing with his father was not paltry to James Boswell. And that postcard or phone call from you can make a child's day.

But I don't get to see my kids for Christmas at all this year, you might be thinking.

Neither do I—not, at least, the three of them who

live seven hundred miles away. They're with me at Christmas only every other year, and this year is the off year. But I'm determined that I will do what I can to make their Christmas as profitable and as enjoyable as I can— from a distance of seven hundred miles. I'm also determined—and I hope you are too—that I won't waste energy or emotion feeling guilty about what I'm not able to do. Rather, remembering that something is better than nothing, I will try to make what I can do as effective and memorable as possible.

We can't give our long-distance children everything we want to give them. It's time we simply admit that to ourselves and take comfort in the things that we *are* able to give them, and then approach those things gratefully and with enthusiasm. It may not be everything, but it's something.

And something is better than nothing.

USE THE TELEPHONE!

You call your kids year-round. Why mention it in a book about Christmas celebrations?

Several reasons. For one, kids who are struggling because they live apart from a parent are going to struggle even more during the Christmas season, when they see, at friends' houses and on TV, cozy little scenes of "normal" families—intact families. The grieving that they've been doing all year will suddenly intensify. And that's when they'll need you the most—the sound of your voice, your attention, the reminder that you love them and that you consider them to be a part of your life.

Another reason: You're reading this book because you want to make some changes in the ways your family celebrates Christmas. And you love your long-distance children enough to want to make them a part of those changes. How do you communicate this new plan to them? One of the ways, as inadequate as it is, is the telephone.

That's not much of a problem with younger kids. Younger children tend to be enthusiastic about phone calls from an absent parent—their tone of voice, their nonstop talking, the questions about when they'll get to see you again, all communicate to you how important you are to them and how much they love you.

But adolescents often respond to your comments in monosyllables. "Yeah. Okay. Uh-huh. Hunh-uh. Okay. Uh-huh." You get the feeling that they're talking on the phone while they're watching TV, and that they're a whole lot more interested in the TV program than they are in the call. Or in you. So you cast around desperately for something interesting to talk about, and then you say some things you think are pretty stupid, and then you hang up, and afterward you say to yourself, *Why do I even bother?* The next time it's your turn to call, you skip it.

Don't skip it. Teenagers, just as much as younger children, need to know that you're interested in them, and that the two of you still figure in each other's lives. It's common for adolescents who live apart from a parent to grieve the loss of that parent and to struggle psychologically even several years after the disruption of the family.

They need constant reminders that they matter to you, that you love them. Cards, letters, gifts, and visits are great reminders. But between visits, they still need to hear your voice.

Only the long-distance parent knows how expensive those phone calls are. And I'm not talking about dollars; I'm talking about pain. The pain of hearing those voices that are so dear to you, the voices of children you haven't seen or held in so long. The pain of hearing their accounts of school or dance lessons or parties or church activities and realizing how much you're missing of their growing up. The pain of their indifference.

For me one measure of the intensity of this grief is the amount of time it's taking me to write this chapter. I find myself stopping after every sentence or two and drawing into myself, reminded of my own grief, of how much I miss my kids, of my fears concerning what problems they may be facing that I'm not even aware of, of the loneliness of Christmas—or any other holiday— apart from them. I did it twice just in this paragraph.

Long-distance parents need to deal with that grief, work through it (perhaps with the aid of a qualified counselor), and then move on. But that isn't easy, is it, when the objects of that grief are constantly being brought before you—every time you send a child-support check, every time you see their pictures, every time you see another parent laughing and playing with kids the same age as yours, every time you find yourself resenting your stepkids because they have the privilege of living with you and your own biological kids don't. Every time you call them on the phone and hear their voices.

Despite the pain, despite your grief, don't avoid calling your kids. They need to hear the sound of your voice saying, "I love you." Make those phone calls an important part of this Christmas season with your kids—frequent, pleasant, and warm. Here are a few suggestions for how to make these Christmas season phone calls—and the phone calls in all the months thereafter—more enjoyable and productive.

1. Schedule your calls. Call at prearranged times. Do you often have a hard time catching anyone at home when you call? Or do you get a busy signal time after time? Why not agree beforehand on a specific time of the week for your calls—say Friday night at eight or Sunday afternoon at three-thirty? That may help to prevent your ex-spouse's complaints that you call at inconvenient times or interrupt dinner.

2. Make a list. The phone rings, your son or daughter answers, and suddenly you can't think of a thing to talk about. During the long, awkward silences, you feel like an adolescent about to ask for his first date.

No need for that. Before you call, spend a couple of minutes jotting down the list of things you'd like to know about (how school's going, whether his team won the game last Friday, whether her sprained ankle's feeling better) and additional things your child might enjoy discussing (the movie you just saw, plans for next summer's visit, the bad accident you saw on the way home from work yesterday). Use that list as a guide and avoid dead air.

3. Be sensitive. Don't try to keep them on the phone too long. Be sensitive to the needs of their household and of the kids themselves. If they have friends over waiting to play, or if your kids are right in the middle of their favorite TV show, call back later or keep the conversation short. You don't want your kids to think of you as a pest.

4. Talk about feelings. Push yourself to express feelings that may be awkward for you. Have a hard time telling your seventeen-year-old son that you love him? Tell him anyway. Even if he says, "Come on, Dad—I'm a senior in high school!" laugh and say, "Oblige me—I'm your dad. It's allowed."

Tell him because you need to say it. And tell him because he needs to hear it. Bill Sanders, author and speaker, surveyed over five thousand high schoolers to find out what they most wished their parents would do differently. The most common response by far, expressed by over half the teens surveyed, was: "I wish my parents would tell me, 'I love you.'" Those weren't five-year-olds. Those were teenagers. And your own kids, especially the long-distance variety, are no different. Don't just talk about the weather. Say, "I love you, Daughter. You're very important to me. I think about you all the time, and I miss you."

CHOOSING AND GIVING GIFTS

The suggestions for choosing gifts in chapter 4 apply to long-distance parenting as well—with one major addition, and that is that you also want to choose gifts for your long-distance kids that will remind them of you and make them feel close to you during the Christmas season and throughout the year.

It's a good idea, for starters, to talk to your kids several weeks ahead of time and ask them for suggestions. Second step: Talk things over with your ex-spouse to see what he or she is planning to get them, so you don't get the same things. (Remember: Your kids are probably giving the same list to both parents.) Send a check only as a last resort; it can communicate to your kids that you didn't care enough to take the time to shop.

Here are some additional ideas that may help.[2]

1. A magazine subscription. Every month, your son or daughter will remember who provided that magazine—especially if you ask over the phone what was in the magazine that month.

2. An audio-cassette player. That might seem like an odd suggestion, until you consider that you can send your child a custom-made Christmas tape, complete with Christmas music, Christmas stories told or read, greetings from each member of the household (including grandparents, if you can manage it), and personal messages from you to each of your children, affirming them and reminding them of your love and of their place in your heart and in your life. Then follow up with a "tape of the month," including new music you've found and more stories. Younger kids especially will enthusiastically listen to those tapes over and over.

3. Photos. Kids enjoy having wallet-size photos of you. And remember: Photos aren't just for Christmas. Send snapshots of family activities, holidays, new Easter outfits, new cars, and so on throughout the year.

4. Clothes. What's so special about clothes? Just this: Carefully stitch a tag into the clothes that includes a short cross-stitched (or indelibly lettered) message: "I love you. Dad." Then, each time your child chooses to put on that garment, he or she will think of you.

5. Books, tapes, or CDs. These last a long time, and your child is reminded of you every time they're read or heard. And they'll mean even more if you can arrange to have them autographed by the author or artist.

6. Membership. Does your child have a special interest that could be encouraged by membership in some organization? For instance, how about buying a membership in a local museum or science club? If your child is into tricks, how about signing him or her up in a "magic-trick-of-the-month" club? (There are such things, and many others for a variety of interests.) If this membership will require activity on your ex-spouse's part, such as driving the child back and forth, you'd better discuss it first. (That's better than arguing about it later and discovering that your gift won't even be used because of lack of cooperation.)

7. Lessons. Dance lessons, piano lessons, baseball camps—all of these are things that stretch kids and also remind them, every time they participate, of the long-distance parent who cared enough to pay for those lessons. But once again, check with the custodial parent first.

8. Video tapes. If your child has a VCR and you have a camcorder, you're in great shape to use one of most kids' favorite technologies. Send light, funny, and warm videos of yourself telling stories or giving puppet shows; send footage from your favorite home videos of the year—fishing trips, babies, holidays, vacations, and so on, *especially* of those activities that included the long-distance child. Just for laughs, throw in a few clips from your child's favorite comedy TV shows, cartoons, or commercials. Or, for teenagers, a couple of videos of favorite rock groups. And this is an idea you can come back to throughout the year. Send a video every two or three months, rather than just once a year.

9. Arrangements for their next visit to you. Kids are uneasy if they don't know when they'll see you next. Put their minds at ease by including in their Christmas gifts some evidence of that next visit, maybe airline tickets or a brochure about places you'll visit. Mention—in your Christmas card or a phone call—some of the plans you're making for that visit and ask what types of things they'd like to do.

10. Flowers. Send flowers? Sure. Girls of all ages, as well as many boys, like receiving flowers. How about a special Christmas bouquet or poinsettia, delivered just before Christmas? (And even kids who genuinely couldn't care less about flowers won't complain about having a box of candy delivered.)

11. Stamped stationery. It's great to get little notes, letters, or drawings from your long-distance kids during the year. You can encourage that by giving them some stationery, preaddressed to yourself and stamped. All they have to do is write or draw on it, seal it, and give it to Mom or Dad to mail with the bills. Most kids love mail, both sending it and getting it, so they'll think it's a great gift. But don't address *all* the envelopes to yourself, just some of them. Your child might also choose to write to other relatives or friends.

12. Hobbies. If your child has a hobby such as collecting stamps or baseball cards or building an HO train set, make part of your Christmas gift sending pieces for that collection. If you think your child might be interested in starting a collection, get a starter set for Christmas. On a recent trip through a museum of natural history, my two youngest sons were fascinated by the mineral displays. When I told them that there are rock collectors' maps showing mineral deposits in each state, they excitedly asked for one. A good gift idea. Similarly, if your child is interested in science, how about a science kit? There's even a subscription you can get for a kit that arrives by monthly installment.[3]

13. School supplies. That might seem like an odd suggestion; why remind them of school during Christmas break? But many kids (hey, don't laugh—I was one) enjoy shiny new pencils and pens and rulers, crisp new binders and folders, and untouched pads of paper. Or how about calculators or software for the older kids? Remember, the idea is to give them something that reminds them often of you.

14. Team paraphernalia. If your son or daughter is a sports fan, for a little extra trouble you can really score some points. Just write (well ahead of time) to the team he or she likes best and ask for autographed photos of the team or of favorite team members. Caps or jerseys with the team name make great gifts, too, especially autographed. If you don't have time to request these items from the team office, most cities have at least one sports specialty shop that carries photos, mementos, caps and clothing, posters, and so on. Even a nonautographed Cubs jersey is better than no Cubs jersey at all.

15. Calendar. If your kids aren't likely to get calendars from Grandma and Grandpa or some other relative, send them yourself, chosen for each child's interests: baseball, horses, cats, boats, art. Your child will look at that calendar several times a month and be reminded of you.

16. Scrapbook. Kids love to look at family photos and at photos of themselves when they were small. Put together a scrapbook (complete with captions, if you have the time) of photos: yourself as a child, wedding pictures of Grandma and Grandpa, and favorite photos of your kids when they were small. Leave plenty of blank pages so your child can add more photos; send more during the year. Then, when your son or daughter feels far from you, there's always the scrapbook.

17. Bible. Giving your kids good-quality, age-appropriate Bibles is one way to encourage their spiritual development, especially if you're concerned that they're not being adequately instructed about God. And send along a couple of good Bible reference books for kids.[4]

WRITE!

You know how kids love to receive mail. Don't disappoint them this Christmas. Make sure that each long-distance child gets a card from you in addition to whatever presents you send. And make the cards something special; make them yourself, if you're talented that way. Personalize them. Write little notes or include clippings of your child's favorite things: horses, cars, sports, or music.

Then carry that habit through the year. Write to your children often and send them cards for other holidays as well: Valentine's Day and Easter, for example. Choose a distinctive stationery, so that your kids will instantly recognize your letters.

Have a hard time thinking of what to write? Watch for articles or news features of items of interest to your long-distance kids—stories about their favorite athletes or animals or actors or hobbies or professions. Then just enclose the clipping and make a short comment about it. That will make it clear to your kids that you're thinking about them, even between letters.

INCLUDE THEM IN YOUR CHRISTMAS

Include your long-distance kids in your Christmas activities, even if they can't be there. For instance: If you're planning to celebrate Christmas a little differently this year—by sponsoring a child in another country, perhaps—explain that to your long-distance kids just as you would if they were at your house. Begin to discuss it with them weeks ahead of time, so they have time to get used to the idea. Give them the opportunity to contribute some of their own money to that child's support, if they want. When you have photos of that child, make sure all the kids, local and long-distance, have a copy. Give them the chance to write to the child.

If you're having a family get-together on Christmas, but some of the kids won't be there, make a phone call to them during the day when all the relatives are around. Let your kids talk to Grandma and Grandpa or a favorite aunt or uncle or cousin. Or have the whole gang gather around the phone to sing a Christmas carol and shout out "Merry Christmas!" to the child who couldn't come. That child will feel included and special.

You won't have time to do all of the things in this chapter for your long-distance kids this Christmas. Don't let that become yet another cause of guilt for you. No chapter in a book, and no parent or ex-spouse, can tell you what is appropriate for you to do for your long-distance children at Christmas or at any other time. You know your own situation, and therefore it's up to you to decide how much of your money and effort and time this Christmas season should go into your long-distance children.

No matter how much you do for them, it won't be everything you'd like to. But it will be something.

And something is better than nothing.

Chapter Eleven

Making It All Work

I'M NO PSYCHIC, but let me tell you something about yourself. First, you're unhappy about the way Christmas is celebrated in our society and in your own family. For years now you've wanted to find some way to change that. But every year's been the same round of exhaustion and disappointment.

You've liked some of the ideas you've read in this book, but how do you go about it? Your spouse—will he or she agree with you? And what about the kids? What will they say about sharing your family's Christmas money with others who need it more—if it means no new Nintendo games?

That's what this chapter is about: how to get your family started on a new kind of Christmas. But let's start with a couple of principles that should apply to all of your Christmas planning. And the first is this: *Something is better than nothing.*

Sound familiar? It was the title of chapter 10. But it also applies to parents who get excited about making changes in the ways their families celebrate Christmas. It's easy to get *so* excited and make *so* many changes that you exhaust and frustrate (and possibly alienate) yourself and your family.

Better to choose those things that you think are most important and that you can accomplish in reasonable, relaxed fashion. And if that means that a lot of things you want to try just don't get done this Christmas, repeat what Chicago Cubs fans say at the end of every baseball season: There's always next year.

The second principle is so important I'm going to put it in a paragraph all its own, and set it in italics:

Start early.

Big surprise, right? You knew that was coming. And you're probably thinking, *Oh, great. If I have to start early to do this stuff, I'll never get it done. I try to start Christmas early every year, and every year I still end up doing everything at the last minute, shopping late, and wrapping presents into the wee hours in the week before Christmas. Forget it.*

Relax. This year, do only the things you have time to do right. Save the rest for next year. Something is better than nothing.

When are you reading this book? (You see, I told you I wasn't a psychic. If I were, I'd have known the answer to that.) September? Then you probably have time to make just about any change I've suggested. Changes in family traditions, such as the family dinner involving all the relatives? September is probably early enough to contact them about that. Want to start preparing the kids for giving up some of their presents so you'll have money to help the needy? No problem. Plenty of time.

Reading in October? You might find that some family members already have nonrefundable tickets to fly in for the Christmas holidays. Oops. Too late. Suggest some changes in the family dinner for *next* year. But you've still got plenty of time to adopt a Compassion child. Do what you can; don't worry about what you can't. Something is better than nothing.

Is it November already? Better start talking to your kids right away if you want them to be excited (rather than resentful) about these changes. And you probably still have presents to buy; chapter 4 might help you in selecting those. That's something. And something is better than nothing.

It's December! You're in a panic about Christmas, so you picked up this book to give you some ideas, and now you see that most of the ideas you like will take more time than you've got left. So what? Pick a few of the simpler ones and use them this year; mark the others that appeal to you to try next year.

But regardless of when you decide to restructure your family's Christmas celebration, initiating those changes requires four areas of participation: making an action plan, deciding about gifts, dealing with others (extended family members, church, organizations), and preparing your kids.

MAKING AN ACTION PLAN

Making Christmas a time of rejoicing and worship instead of the overcommercialized, high-anxiety trauma it too often is requires a *conscious decision* and a *plan.*

The decision is yours to make. If the opportunities outlined in this book excite you, then resolve to make this a watershed Christmas for your family, one that will change the way your family celebrates Christ's birth forever.

If you're a single parent, that decision is as simple as making it. You decide, and that's it. If you're married, then of course it has to be a joint decision. And, as with many of the joint decisions in your marriage, that may not be easy. Especially if your spouse isn't into reading or just doesn't have the time to read this book early enough to get a good jump on the holidays or is stubborn enough to put off reading it just because you happen to suggest it.

If that's the case, find a time when the two of you can just talk about some of the ideas from this book that appeal to you. If your spouse's response is enthusiastically positive, or at least supportive of your own concerns, you're ready to make a plan. If your spouse seems indifferent, suggest a couple of the simpler options for this year and see if he or she will agree to give them a try, as an experiment, with the option of making more sweeping changes next year.

With that decision made, you need a plan—one that will excite and involve your family. And here's where the red flags go up.

There are two kinds of people in this world: those who carry Daytimers ("brain books") in which they organize every detail of their lives, and those who don't. Or maybe you'd prefer to divide it into those who balance their checkbook (right down to the penny) every month, and those who don't. Or those who make lists before they go to the store, and those who don't. Choose any of the above. The point is, some people take an almost militaristic approach to the organization of their personal lives, and some people prefer to stroll through life, inefficient but happy.

I'm not attempting to change the type of person you are. If you're the kind of person whose eyes lit up when you saw the word *plan* and who keeps your Daytimer on your keychain, go to it. Map out every decision that needs to be made, whom you need to talk to and when; set a schedule for every step of every action you plan to take and then memo everybody involved (and be sure to keep file copies). That approach works just fine. You'll be able to accomplish the changes I've talked about in this book, and your family's Christmas will benefit.

And then there are the people who simply won't do something if it requires a lot of detailed planning. If that's you, never fear. That approach will work too. If you're more comfortable with an informal—even indefinite—plan, then take that approach.

Either way, your plan needs to include two things: (1) a decision on which elements of your family's Christmas celebration you want to adjust and (2) an awareness of the steps necessary to accomplish that, and when they need to be done.

For instance: One of the things that bothers you about Christmas is its commercialism and materialism, and the greed in your own kids that's encouraged by those aspects. You want to encourage them to think about someone else's needs. You've decided to adopt a Compassion child as a Christmas gift from the whole family to the whole family. With that decided, you need to know that the agency you work through to adopt this child will need at least a month to process your application and assign a child and send a photo. So, if you want a name and photo by Christmas, you should submit your application before Thanksgiving.

Even planning at that simple level may sound discouraging to some of you who are already dreading the holidays because they're always so hectic. *That's all I need—one more responsibility, one more thing to sit down and do,* you might be thinking. Remember that the purpose behind all of this isn't to make your Christmas more hectic or busier—just the opposite. The point is to get your Christmas under control and make it more enjoyable, and more honoring to Christ, for your whole family. A few minutes of planning is worth that.

If you're into forms, I've included a simple one on the following pages that might help you to make plans for the holidays—unless you're a dedicated Daytimer user, in which case your Daytimer probably already *has* a form for planning holidays.

A CHRISTMAS PLANNER

New Activity or Approach You Want to Try	Purpose of This Change	People Who Must Be Consulted	Steps Necessary to Accomplish This Change	Deadline for Each Step

If you're not into forms, just skip it, and forget I even brought it up.

GIVING THOUGHT TO GIFTS

Chapters 4 and 5 discussed what kinds of gifts to give to whom, and when to give them. If you're creative and thoughtful in choosing those gifts, you'll need to do a little advance planning—or at least advance thinking.

For example, magazines. My son gets *Sports Illustrated for Kids;* another son and two daughters get *World.* Good choices for their particular interests and personalities, personally selected to celebrate for each of those kids who they are. But you don't think of that on December 22 and have anything to show for it on December 25. You subscribe weeks ahead of time, if you want a little gift card to wrap and put under the tree or the January issue arriving in time to wrap.

Other gifts may have to be ordered through the mail; others made. Include in your planning enough time to choose, order, or arrange for any gifts that require extra time beyond a quick trip to Penney's the week before Christmas.

The more creative and thoughtful you want to be, the more likely you are to find that the gifts you choose require extra planning. Not necessarily extra *time* on your part—after all, those last-week trips to the shopping centers, fighting traffic and crowds and long lines, take plenty of time, too—but extra planning. Spend an hour in October rather than two hours on December 23.

INITIATING CONTACTS OUTSIDE THE FAMILY

The more adventurous you become in rethinking Christmas, the more cooperation you'll need from people outside your immediate family. Perhaps an ex-spouse who'll have to agree to a somewhat different arrangement for Christmas visitation or to a plan for a creative gift (such as dance lessons). Or parents and other relatives who need to agree to a little different approach to a family get-together. Or church members who have never gone caroling before and think it might be a lot of work. Or an urban ministry to the homeless, to arrange for you and your family to work in their shelter one day during Christmas week.

Many of those contacts and negotiations will be relatively easy; others, especially involving family members, may be difficult. It isn't easy to persuade conservative people to change the way they do things, especially when "We've always done it this way; it just won't seem like Christmas."

And that's why you need to begin early. When you're deciding which activities to try this year, remember that those requiring participation or permission from people outside your immediate family may take longer to prepare for than you think. And if you try to force their agreement, you'll only frustrate them as well as yourself. Once you've decided what you'd like this year's activities to include, start laying the groundwork.

Here's an approach that may work. Make the initial contact and suggest your alternative: "What would you think of skipping the family gift exchange this year and spending the money instead to all get together for a weekend somewhere? I'd rather have the time together than the goodies anyway." If you sense resistance, try this approach: "Well, think about it, okay? It's just an idea. We'll go ahead the traditional way this year, and when we're all together for the Christmas dinner, I'll bring it up and we can talk about it for next year." It's an approach that works with church members and friends as well as family. People are often uncomfortable if they feel you're trying to cram your ideas down their throat or if they don't have time to get used to a new idea. There's no rush.

Don't overwork and frustrate yourself; bite off only what you can chew. Remember the Cubs: There's always next year.

PREPARING YOUR KIDS

"Well, kids," you say with a sly smile on Christmas Eve, "I've got some great news. This year we really want to emphasize the true meaning of Christmas. We want to relate to the world with the compassion of Christ. We don't want to fall into the world's trap of materialism. We want to put the Christ back in Christmas!"

"Super, Dad!" your fifteen-year-old daughter chirps. "Really neat! I was, you know, like thinking the same thing myself."

"Great!" you affirm. "And that's why we're each going to have only one present under the tree tomorrow morning. The rest of the money—that we would have spent on cheap toys that would just break anyway or clothes we don't need—we've used to help people who really need our help. Poor people. In this country and in other countries too."

"Hey, great!" your ten-year-old son says. "Can I help choose which countries? And I've got some old toys they can have too."

"You know, Dad," your daughter says, "I was thinking. Aren't there some places downtown that, like, serve food and stuff to bag ladies and stuff like that? Wouldn't it be neat to go down there and help out tomorrow? You know, dish out soup and stuff? Instead of just staying here and like really pigging out on turkey and pumpkin pie and stuff when people are starving?"

"Excellent idea!" you cry. "Let's call and volunteer for it right now!"

Right. As your daughter would say, *Get real, Dad*. A more likely scenario:

"WHAT?" your son and daughter say in unison. "We're going to have *how* many presents under the tree?"

"Well," you explain, "I just feel that, with people in need all around us, it would be more in keeping with the spirit of Christmas—"

"Does this mean I don't get that green sweater?" your daughter shouts. "Because that was at the top of my list! I need that sweater!"

"Well," you hedge, "I don't really want to spoil your surprise for tomorrow morning. But your mother and I felt that, if we were going to buy only one present for each of you, it should be something that really affirms the wonderful person you are, and emphasizes—"

"I didn't get the sweater?" she screams. "Now what am I going to wear to the Winter Festival? How can I—"

"Hey, it's okay, Dad," your son assures you. "We know you get these ideas sometimes. It's all right. You're a generous person. It's just that this one is a *bad idea,* Dad! This is Christmas! We've been waiting for this for months! We want to wake up tomorrow to a tree full of goodies! Now go get that money you were going to give to the poor and go out to the mall—"

"Well," you say, "actually, you see, I've already sent the money to some missions organizations and to some needy families our church supports and—"

You stop, appalled at the expressions of shock on your children's faces. Moments of silence.

"The money's gone?" your daughter whispers.

"Gone," you say.

"Gone?" says your son.

You nod your head. They sit quietly for a moment, and then, wiping their eyes, exit slowly—your fifteen-year-old throwing you one last look as she exits, a look that only fifteen-year-olds possess.

Don't kid yourself: If you want to change the way your family celebrates Christmas, you have to start early.

As soon as you (or you and your spouse, if you're married) have the new plan for Christmas even sketchily mapped out, it's time to start discussing these new ideas with the kids. And you may be surprised at their response—they might be far more receptive than you expect. The new activities you suggest—caroling, volunteering time in soup kitchens, delivering Christmas baskets to needy families—might sound exciting to them.

And (as long as they realize that Christmas will still be a time of gift giving, and that they won't be cut off the receiving end entirely) you may find them excited about sharing your family's plenty with others who have little. My kids, frankly, are more interested in our Compassion child than I am. They mention him more often and probably look at his picture more often and with more focused thought than I do. They pray for him every night, and, if I forget to mention him in our prayers at mealtime, they remind me. All of this even though they know that the monthly checks we send him cut into the amount of cash we have available for our own entertainment and for gift giving.

If your kids have a chance to help choose the new Christmas plan, they'll feel more ownership of it. Give them several options; let them choose the things that appeal to them most. Generally kids are excited about new experiences—as long as they don't feel that their interests are being ignored or their security threatened (and remember that such things as Christmas turkey dinners with relatives are definitely part of your child's security). If not all of your children live with you year-round, find a way to include the nonresidential children in the discussion—either by phone or during a visit.

The Alternate Celebrations Catalogue includes these suggestions for involving your kids in the planning:

> On 3 x 5 cards I write a "sentence stub" which each person at the table must complete. Some that we've used are:

The best thing that happened to me today was. . .

The nicest thing about Christmas is . . .

The thing that worries me the most is . . .

Another strategy we use to provoke discussion is "Fantasy." Some of the Fantasy situations we've proposed are:

◇ If you won the $1 million lottery, what would you do with the money?

◇ If you could not spend any money at Christmas time, what kind of gifts could you give?

◇ If you had all the toys and clothes you could possibly want, what then would you want for [Christmas]?

Another strategy we use involves "Ranking"— prioritizing our needs and wants and desires:

List in order the five things you want most to happen at Christmas.

Which of these would be the worst for you?

◇ to have to go to church on Christmas eve

◇ to do without new toys on Christmas

◇ to make Christmas gifts instead of buying them

What is the most important thing about Christmas?

◇ remembering Jesus' birthday

◇ giving and receiving gifts

◇ family and friends getting together[1]

If you use this approach, make sure that everyone has a chance to present personal views and that those views are listened to respectfully and nonjudgmentally.

It isn't necessary to set up a weekly family meeting—Thursday evening at nine, after Jon finishes his seventy-five minutes of homework and all the supper dishes, rinsed, are in their proper places in the dishwasher and the dog has been fed and walked—to talk about these changes. You can talk about them with your kids over dinner or in the car on the way to the ball game. Doesn't matter. The important thing is to talk with the kids, get them involved, and then initiate whatever you've chosen to initiate early enough to get it done before Christmas without having to stay up all night.

If you discuss the plan with them early enough, anticipate cooperation and even enthusiasm from the kids.

If you wait until the last minute to bring them into the plan, expect a scene.

BE FLEXIBLE

And after all this planning and preparation, what happens if your plan fails? What happens if your family grumbles about the "old" things they missed because you didn't do them this year, about the "boring" new things you tried? What happens if *you,* when the season's over, realize you just didn't enjoy it as much as you thought you would?

You think through what went wrong and make adjustments for next year. Don't be discouraged. Changing your family's patterns of celebrating Christmas isn't a one-time shot, an all-or-nothing deal. It's a process that lasts a lifetime, sifting through old traditions and new opportunities, capitalizing on the changing interests and abilities of your children as they grow, responding to changes in society.

What is more dynamic than a family? Shouldn't family celebrations be dynamic too?

Your family's Christmas celebration, if it's like most, is more accident than anything else—a haphazard collection of combined family traditions, odds and ends picked up from here and there, and a hodge-podge of cultural influences designed more to separate you from your cash than anything else. Yet we cling to that accidental conglomerate because we've become comfortable with it. The law of inertia applies—a family Christmas celebration sunk in a morass of materialistic tedium tends to remain in a morass of materialistic tedium. Interpretation: Some of the new things you try probably *won't* go over with your family. Resolve not to be discouraged.

The key is to be flexible. In your initial planning this year, and in your "revised" planning next year, your goal is a plan that the whole family will own—not one you've imposed on them against their will. That means you'll have to compromise. Your spouse and kids might think some of your new ideas are pretty ho-hum. But they'll be excited about other things you didn't even think of and may not care about at all. Give and take. Make sure everybody wins in putting this plan together.

When you've settled on a personal family plan for this Christmas, announce it clearly to all the family. Make sure everyone, even the youngest, understands how it will work and how it will affect all of you. Make it sound exciting—because it is.

It's exciting because it will be both fun and meaningful. It's exciting because your family has chosen *against* the dominant values of a godless society. And it's exciting because your family, unlike that innkeeper of long ago, is making room for Jesus on his birthday.

Conclusion

AS AN UNDERGRADUATE I was fascinated when I discovered first *The Hobbit* and then the whole Lord of the Rings trilogy by J. R .R. Tolkien. I read and reread those books, feeling a little guilty to be, as an adult, deriving such joy from reading what seemed to be fairy tales—a little like the adults in TV commercials who gobble Kellogg's Frosted Flakes in secret.

I think I'd finished my second complete reading of the set of four books before I realized why they so appealed to me (beyond the general excellence of Tolkien's writing). Tolkien, a Christian, had created a wonderful vehicle for describing in tangible terms the largely intangible battle between good and evil—the battle between those of us who, apparently against all odds, remain loyal to our Creator, and the principalities and powers against whom we wrestle. Among the freeway traffic and tax forms, I have often lost sight of the battlefield scenes in Revelation. But, reading Tolkien, I once again felt myself part of something much larger than the petty struggles of modern life; I realized that I was not only a world Christian but a cosmic Christian, a true soldier in the only war that really matters.

A few years later I happened across an essay of Tolkien's in which he described one of the purposes of fantasy as *recovery*—meaning recovery of a proper, wholistic world view, a world view that includes spiritual reality, rather than being limited to the merely empirical reality we so often mistake for the whole show.

I encourage you to view your Christmas celebration in those terms. There is more at stake than merely getting more organized, than enjoying the holiday more. It *is* a battle. This *is* a struggle—*the* struggle—between good and evil. Between God and evil. And the territory over which we are fighting has long been held by the enemy.

You and your family can reclaim that territory for Christ. And the struggle through which you will reclaim it is just as noble, just as praiseworthy, as Frodo's lonely journey at the end of Tolkien's trilogy to destroy the ring of power. And even more crucial, because it is real.

I'm cheering for you. And you will need those cheers and prayers, because there will be forces arrayed against you to cause you to fail—through discouragement, strife within your family, busyness, distractions, even greed. But with God's help, you can prevail. You can establish for your family, within that vast stronghold of Satan, a little outpost of worship and peace and thanksgiving and generosity and compassion.

And it won't be the only outpost. Other families have done the same thing, and more will join you—little points of light in the darkness, here and there, like stars in a dark sky. One family at a time.

And from those tiny points of light will come a song, faint at first, then stronger and stronger:

> *O come to us, abide with us,*
> *Our Lord Emmanuel.*

Until the light overpowers the darkness.
Happy birthday to you, Lord Jesus.

Notes

Chapter One: Why Christmas Matters

1. John MacArthur, *God with Us: The Miracle of Christmas* (Grand Rapids: Zondervan, 1989), 8–9.
2. "No Christmas, No Halloween, No Prayer," *Youthworker Update* 2, no. 9 (May 1988): 6.
3. "We Wish You a Merry . . . Er, Winter," *Youthworker Update* 2, no. 4 (December 1987): 5.
4. Walter Wangerin, Jr., *The Book of the Dun Cow* (New York: Pocket Books, 1979), 22.
5. Paul Pearsall, *Power of the Family: Strength, Comfort, and Healing* (Garden City, N.Y.: Doubleday, 1990).

Chapter Two: The Spirit of Christmas Present

1. Kenneth S. Kantzer, "Ron Sider Is Mostly Right," *Christianity Today* (October 8, 1990): 21. Copyright © *Christianity Today*, 1990. Used by permission.
2. John Kavanaugh, "Idols of the Marketplace," *Media&Values* (Fall 1986). Published by the Center for Media and Values, Los Angeles. Used by permission.
3. Jeffrey Zaslow, from an article in the *Wall Street Journal* (March 13, 1987). Quoted in *Youthworker Update* 1, no. 8 (April 1987): 3.
4. "Shameful Bequests to the Next Generation," *Time* (October 8, 1990): 45. Copyright © The Time Inc. Magazine Company. Reprinted by permission.
5. Quoted in "TV Violence on the Upswing," *Media Update* (May-June 1990): 7.

Chapter Three: A Biblical Christmas: Honoring the Party Child

1. O. Henry, "The Gift of the Magi," *The Four Million* (New York: Doubleday, Page, & Company, 1906), 24–25.
2. A. W. Tozer, *Worship: The Missing Jewel of the Evangelical Church* (Harrisburg, Pa.: Christian Publications, n.d.), 12–13.
3. Other possibilities include Matt. 1:18–24 and 2:13–23; Luke 1:26–56 and 2:21–40; John 1:1–5 and 3:16–21; and Phil. 2:5–11.
4. The following books offer dozens of suggestions for bringing Scripture to life in your family Bible reading times: Paul T. Johnson, *Family Fusion* (London: Scripture Union, 1991); Alice Chapin, *Building Your Child's Faith* (Nashville: Thomas Nelson, 1990); Marshall Shelley, ed., *Keeping Your Kids Christian* (Ann Arbor: Servant, 1990).
5. David Lambert, "My Dumb Sister and the Crazy Shepherds," *Virtue* (December 1982).
6. Anthony Campolo, *Growing Up in America: A Sociology of Youth Ministry* (Grand Rapids: Zondervan, 1989), 145.

Chapter Four: And a Partridge in a Pear Tree: Choosing Gifts

1. MacArthur, *God with Us,* 129.
2. Alice Slaikeu Lawhead, *The Christmas Survival Book* (Batavia, Ill.: Lion Publishing, 1990), 94. Copyright © 1990 by Alice Slaikeu Lawhead. Used by permission.

Chapter Five: When Is Christmas?

1. Milo Shannon-Thornberry, *The Alternate Celebrations Catalogue* (New York: The Pilgrim Press, 1982), 96.
2. Sharon Lee, *Joyous Days: A Collection of Advent and Christmas Activities* (Minneapolis: Winston Press, 1984), 60, 65, 76. Copyright © 1984 by Winston Press, Inc. Reprinted by permission of HarperCollins Publishers.
3. Lawhead, *The Christmas Survival Book,* 207–8.
4. Mala Powers, *Follow the Year: A Family Celebration of Christian Holidays.* (New York: Harper and Row, 1985), 48.

5. Quoted in "A Peek through the Keyhole," by Evelyn Bence, in *Today's Christian Woman* (November/December, 1985): 45.

Chapter Six: Thanks for the Memories
1. Quoted in Bence, "A Peek Through the Keyhole," 42–43.

Chapter Seven: Sharing Christmas with Family and Friends
1. Ole Rijs, "Trends in Danish Religion," *Social Compass* 35 (1988): 45–53. Quoted in *The Family in America* (February 1989): 4.
2. Some activities are suggested in Lawhead, *The Christmas Survival Book* and Shannon-Thornberry, *The Alternate Celebrations Catalogue*.
3. Lawhead, *The Christmas Survival Book*, 133.

Chapter Eight: Exporting Christmas: Sharing with Strangers
1. Ernest Becker, *The Denial of Death* (New York: The Free Press, 1975). Quoted in Campolo, *Growing Up in America*, 33.
2. Campolo, *Growing Up in America*, 33–34.
3. Kantzer, "Ron Sider Is Mostly Right," 21.
4. Nancy Roberts, "Can Parents Make Justice a Family Tradition?" *Salt* (September 1986).
5. "Doing Good as a Family Tradition," *Youthworker Update* 1, no. 3 (November 1986), 7–8.
6. Quoted in Bence, "A Peek through the Keyhole," 42.
7. Quoted in Bence, "A Peek through the Keyhole," 45.
8. Shannon-Thornberry, *The Alternate Celebrations Catalogue*, 89.
9. Marlene LeFever, "18 Great Ways to Light 'Em Up!" *Christian Parenting Today* (November-December 1991).
10. You'll find lots of Christmas games and activities suitable for young children in Lee, *Joyous Days: A Collection of Advent and Christmas Activities* and Sarah Liu and Mary Lou Vittitow, *Fun Things for Kids at Christmastime* (Cincinnati: Standard Publishing, 1991).
11. Lawhead, *The Christmas Survival Book*, 158.
12. For a more complete list of social action agencies, see Anthony Campolo, *Ideas for Social Action*, rev. ed. (Grand Rapids: Zondervan, 1991), chap. 7.

Chapter Nine: How to Pick a Gift for Your Spouse
1. Gary Jackson Oliver, "Growing Healthy Marriages," *Focal Point* 10, no. 4 (October-December 1990): 3–4.
2. Ibid.
3. Suggestions: H. Norman Wright, *How to Speak Your Spouse's Language* (Old Tappan, N.J.: Fleming H. Revell, 1986); Bill and Lynne Hybels, *Fit to Be Tied* (Grand Rapids: Zondervan, 1991); Ed Wheat, M.D., *Love Life for Every Married Couple* (Grand Rapids: Zondervan, 1980); H. Norman Wright, *Communication: Key to Your Marriage* (Ventura, Calif.: Regal Books, 1974).
4. Wright, *Communication: Key to Your Marriage,* 188–89. Copyright © 1974 Regal Books. Used by permission.

Chapter Ten: Long-Distance Christmases: Something Is Better Than Nothing
1. David Lambert, "Making Memories with Dad," *Christian Parenting Today* (September-October 1988), 74.
2. Some suggestions from George Newman, *101 Ways to Be a Long-Distance Super-Dad* (Saratoga, Calif.: Blossom Valley Press, 1981).
3. *Things of Science* (R.D. 1, Box 130, Newtown, PA 18940).
4. Suggestions: *International Children's Bible Dictionary* by Lynn Waller (Dallas: Word, 1989); *How Do We Know the Bible Is True?* by Lynn Waller (Grand Rapids: Zondervan, 1991).

Chapter Eleven: Making It All Work
1. Shannon-Thornberry, *The Alternate Celebrations Catalogue,* 53–54.